Documents on British
Political History

Book Two   1815–1914

Documents on British Political History
by JOHN WROUGHTON

Book One 1688–1815
Book Three 1914–1970 [IN PREPARATION]

Documents on British Economic and Social History
by PETER LANE

Book One 1750–1870
Book Two 1870–1939
Book Three 1945–1967

SOURCES OF HISTORY SERIES
Cromwell and the Roundheads by JOHN WROUGHTON
Smuggling by JOHN PAXTON and JOHN WROUGHTON
Plots, Traitors and Spies by JOHN WROUGHTON

Documents on British Political History

History

Book Two 1815–1914

JOHN WROUGHTON, M.A., F.R.Hist.S.
Senior History Master
King Edward's School
Bath

MACMILLAN

First published 1971
Reprinted 1973

Published by
MACMILLAN EDUCATION LIMITED
London and Basingstoke
Companies and representatives
throughout the world

Printed in Great Britain by
FLETCHER AND SON LTD, NORWICH

Contents

Acknowledgements

The publishers wish to thank The Radio Times Hulton Picture Library for kind permission to reproduce the illustrations throughout the book.

1 The Corn Laws, 1815

That the great and sudden depreciation in the value of the produce of their farms has reduced many of the petitioners to a situation of great difficulty and distress: That the expence which now attends the cultivation of poor and middling land exceeds the present value of its produce; and that unless some effectual remedy is applied, many of the petitioners will no longer be able to pay their rents and taxes, and the greater part of the lands in occupation of the petitioners must be wholly abandoned, and a great proportion of their labourers and servants must be thrown out of employment: The petitioners are sensible, that if the greatest part of their present rents was abated, it would afford a very inadequate remedy to the evil, since the average of rents in Cleveland, as the petitioners apprehend, does not exceed one-fifth part of their annual expences: The petitioners beg leave very respectfully to state, that they conceive the grievance under which they labour to arise from the immoderate importation of foreign corn: That the petitioners are subject to the burden of Poor Rates, Taxes, Tithes and various Assessments unknown to and not felt by the foreign growers of corn; and the petitioners humbly conceive it is unfair and impolitic to suffer these foreigners to have the command of the British market: The petitioners also humbly conceive that corn is properly to be classed amongst the articles of British manufacture, and is entitled both in reason and justice to the same protecting duties in the home market; ...

Petition of the Occupiers of Farms in Cleveland,
February 1815

8

Comment

The Peace of Paris of 1814 ended not only the wars against France, but also a period of great prosperity for British farmers. Import of corn during the war had been made almost impossible by Napoleon's Continental System. Farmers quickly took advantage of the high prices brought about by the shortage. Farms were expanded; land was enclosed and improved; whole new areas of poor, waste ground were brought under the plough. Then suddenly, in 1814, the enormous profits ceased as cheap foreign corn again flooded into the country. Prices fell rapidly and many farmers, who had committed themselves to high rents and expensive machinery, were ruined. As a result Lord Liverpool's government, which largely represented the landowning interest, passed the Corn Law in 1815. This banned the import of foreign corn until the price of British corn had reached 80 shillings a quarter. The cost of bread inevitably remained high.

Questions

a. Why had the value of farm produce dropped so suddenly by 1815?

b. Why had the petitioners bothered to cultivate 'poor and middling land' in the first place?

c. What three consequences did the petitioners fear in the absence of immediate government action?

d. Why were foreigners in a better position to sell their corn more cheaply than English farmers?

e. What remedy did the petitioners request? What argument did they use to support this?

f. Why did they feel that their poverty had not been caused by high rents?

g. Discuss the advantages and disadvantages of the Corn Laws from the point of view of (i) the farmers, (ii) ordinary workers, (iii) factory-owners.

h. Why do you think that parliament reacted favourably to petitions like this?

2 Suspension of Habeas Corpus, 1817

The petitions to Parliament from the different agricultural interests were numerous this year [1816]. The manufacturers at the same time complained of that want of employment which was occasioned by the general impoverishment of their countrymen; and riots arose in the inland counties. At the close of the year, a popular meeting took place in Spa-fields, Islington, and resolutions of reform, suggested by Mr. Henry Hunt, were voted by acclamation. The rioters, parading the streets, carried off fire-arms from the shops of several gunsmiths; and Watson's son shot at, and desperately wounded an individual in Mr. Beckwith's shop, Snow-hill. The mob now marched to the Royal Exchange, where they had a short contest with the Lord Mayor.

The opening of Parliament in 1817 was anticipated, therefore, with anxiety . . . on the return of the Prince from the House of Peers, an immense crowd had assembled in the Park, by whom he was received with marked demonstrations of discontent and anger; on passing Carlton-house, the glass of the carriage was broken by a stone: nor was it without some difficulty that he at length reached the Palace. This flagrant outrage being on the same day reported by Lord Sidmouth to Parliament, the two Houses joined in an address suitable to the occasion; and voted the offer of £1000 reward for the discovery of the offender. . . . On the 24th [February] a motion was made by Lord Sidmouth in the Upper House, for a suspension of the Habeas Corpus Act until the 1st of July ensuing.

This called forth an able speech from the Marquess Wellesley. . . . He blamed the unskilful management of our affairs, particularly our commercial arrangements with foreign countries, which had led to these discontents; and he was not content to place in such unskilful hands the liberties of the people.

Lord Liverpool remarked, that 'They had, according to their report, proofs of a system to overthrow the constitution of the country. . . . He felt the necessity of preserving to every man his fire-side; and on these grounds he asked, for a very short time, the powers which were indispensable to the salvation of the State.'

Memoirs of the Rt. Hon. The Earl of Liverpool, 1827

1 The Peterloo
Massacre, 1819

Comment

By 1817 Britain was in a state of serious depression. Wartime needs had
speeded up the introduction of machinery both on farms and in
factories, causing unemployment in some areas. This growing problem
had been aggravated further by the ending of the war in 1814. De-
mobilised soldiers returned home without jobs. Textile and metal
industries were badly hit by the ending of government contracts.
Farmers were ruined by the arrival of cheap foreign corn. Wages fell,
but the price of bread remained high (see Document 1). Workers
expressed their grievances by strikes, marches, petitions, mass-meetings
and riots. Fearing a revolution, Liverpool's government passed a series
of repressive measures designed to silence these protests. In 1817 it
suspended the Habeas Corpus Act, thereby taking the power to im-
prison suspected trouble-makers without a trial.

Questions

a. Which two groups in the community were clearly suffering distress
   in 1816? Give reasons for this.
b. In what two ways did people express their grievances?
c. What solution to their troubles was proposed by Henry Hunt? Why?
d. Why did Liverpool feel that the suspension of Habeas Corpus was
   necessary?
e. Examine Plate 1 which shows the Peterloo Massacre of 1819. What
   was the meeting about? Why did the authorities take such strong
   action? Does this picture give an accurate impression of what
   actually happened?

3 The Repeal of the Combination Laws, 1824

Mr. Francis Place called in and examined.

Have you had much experience with respect to clubs, and combination of workmen and their employers? — Yes. I was for some years a journeyman myself, and got sadly punished by the masters combining not to employ me; this was for having interfered in a combination of the men. I afterwards formed several clubs, for the purpose of compelling the masters to give an advance of wages. I thought then, and still think it was proper. Wages were very low in some trades, and the workmen had no other means whatever to procure an increase. These combinations of the men were all of them ultimately successful . . .

What is the system the journeymen tailors now pursue? — The system is all but a military system. The orders come from the Executive, and are always obeyed. . . . The whole body never, in any instance, discuss the propriety of a strike, as that would subject them to prosecution under the Combination Laws. Do the men generally know who are the regulators? — No. It is whispered among them that there is to be a strike; but they never discuss the subject: they strike when bid . . .

Do you think the repeal of the Combination Laws would lower wages? — No. I think the wages of journeymen tailors, and other workmen, would be just what they are now, except in some few cases, where the Combination Laws have kept them too low. In general, the men have evaded the law, and set it totally aside. Then the only effect of the Combination Laws has been to create irritated feelings between the masters and men? — Just so . . .

Have you ever known a master prosecuted by the men for combination? — No. I believe it would be nearly impossible to prosecute a master to conviction. To prosecute at all, money must be raised; to raise money there must be a combination amongst the men, and then they may be prosecuted by the masters . . .

If the men could legally combine, disputes would seldom occur, but when they did, they would be settled by compromise between the parties. Workmen dread a strike. . . . The influence of the women in the case of a strike, is of much importance; they never consent, but in extreme cases . . .

Minutes of Select Committee on Artizans and Machinery, February 1824

Comment

By 1822 Britain's trade had started to improve, the depression was slowly lifting and times were becoming better even for the working classes. As the tension eased, the Tory government gradually relaxed. In 1822 Liverpool reshaped his cabinet and introduced three men who believed in moderate reform — Canning (foreign secretary), Peel (home secretary) and Huskisson (president of the Board of Trade). Among the first to benefit were the trade unions, which had been made illegal by the Combination Laws of 1799–1800. The repeal of these Laws was largely due to the efforts of Francis Place, a London tailor, and Joseph Hume, a radical M.P., who chaired the committee of enquiry set up to investigate. This extract is taken from its report.

Questions

a. What was the main purpose of the clubs and combinations?
b. Why did Place feel that their existence was right and proper?
c. How successful had the Combination Laws been in banning combinations of workmen?
d. What evidence is there here to suppose that the employers, too, had continued to combine against their workers? Why did it prove impossible to prosecute them for this?
e. What undesirable effects had the Combination Laws brought about?
f. What is there to suggest that the journeymen tailors were (i) well organised, (ii) well disciplined?
g. What results did Place expect from the repeal of the Laws? Was he proved right?
h. Why is 'the influence of the women' so important in a strike?

4 Ireland—Catholic Emancipation, 1829

Lord Anglesey to Lord Francis Gower 2 *July 1828*
Such is the extraordinary power of the agitators, that I am quite certain they could lead on the people to open rebellion at a moment's notice, and their organisation is such, that in the hands of desperate and intelligent leaders, they would be extremely formidable. . . . I believe their success inevitable — that no power under heaven can arrest its progress. There may be rebellion, you may put to death thousands, you may suppress it, but it will only put off the day of compromise . . .

But will things remain as they are? Certainly not. They are bad, they must get worse, and I see no possible means of improving them but by depriving the demagogues of the power of directing people. And by taking Messrs. O'Connell, Sheil and the rest of them from the Association, and placing them in the House of Commons, this desirable object would be at once accomplished.

Peel to Colonel Yates *18 February 1829*
The events of the Clare election, with the conviction that the same scenes would be enacted in nearly every county in Ireland if matters were to remain just as they have been for the last five or six years, convinced me that it was not safe for the Protestant interest in Ireland that they should remain so . . .

From Peel's Memoir on the Roman Catholic Relief Bill
The chief difficulty was with the King. . . . To Lord Eldon he had said 'that, if he gave assent to the Roman Catholic Relief Bill, he would go to the Baths abroad, and from them to Hanover; that he would return no more to England, and that his subjects might get a Catholic King in the Duke of Clarence' . . .

I now feared that the difficulties were almost insuperable. There was the declared opinion of the King, the declared opinion of the House of Lords, the declared opinion of the Church, unfavourable to the measures we were disposed to recommend.

Being convinced that the Catholic question must be settled, and without delay. . . . I determined not to insist upon retirement from office, but to make the Duke the voluntary offer of official co-operation . . .
Sir Robert Peel, ed. C. S. Parker, Vol. II, 1899

Comment

In 1828 the Duke of Wellington took over the government. Liverpool had resigned through ill health and Canning, his successor, had died a few months later. Shortly afterwards a crisis broke out in Ireland. Since the Act of Union (1801), Ireland had been ruled over from Westminster. But although Irish Catholics had the right to vote, they were not allowed to sit in the House of Commons. A highly-organised Catholic Association was formed by Daniel O'Connell to campaign for the removal of this restriction (i.e. to gain 'Catholic Emancipation'). In 1828 he successfully fought a by-election in County Clare but was unable, of course, to take his seat. This brought the whole question to a head. Feeling ran high and, under the threat of a serious rebellion, Wellington and Peel reluctantly decided to agree to the demand.

Questions

a. What two main advantages would the Irish movement have possessed in any future rebellion?
b. What is there in these extracts to suggest that Anglesey believed that (i) the use of force would be unsuccessful, (ii) Catholic Emancipation should be granted?
c. What three important bodies in England opposed Emancipation? What reasons do you think they had for this?
d. What had finally convinced Peel that Emancipation was necessary?
e. What position did (i) Peel, (ii) Eldon, (iii) the Duke hold in the Cabinet?
f. Why do you think that Peel had decided originally to retire from office?
g. Why did he change his mind?
h. What do you understand by (i) 'the Association', (ii) 'demagogues'?

2 O'Connell at the head of a band of ruffians. 'Catholic Petitioners or Symptoms of Peaceable Appeal'

3 'Taking my seat'. A cartoon of O'Connell in barrister's wig and gown, published in 1829

O'Connell and the County Clare elections

Comment

These cartoons deal with the crisis in Ireland over Catholic Emancipation, 1828–29. (See Document 4.)

Questions

a. Examine Plate 2.
  (i) How does the cartoonist suggest that O'Connell approved of violent methods?
  (ii) What did the cartoonist fear would happen after Catholic Emancipation had been granted?
b. Examine Plate 3.
  (i) What is the building on the left? Who is the man blocking the entrance? Why?
  (ii) Who are the other characters in the picture?

5 Peel and the Metropolitan Police, 1829

Letter from Peel to Wellington   *29 May 1829*
My dear Duke, — I send you the Report of the Committee of last year on the Police of the Metropolis. . . . In 1822 there were 2,539 committals: in 1825, 2,902; and in 1828, 3,516. This is a strong proof of the rapid increase of crime, and the necessity of some effectual measures for its repression. In 1822 there were 12 committals for breaking into a dwelling house; in 1825, 23: and in 1828, 102.

The paper marked A contains a list of parishes in which the watch establishment is defective. Just conceive the state of one parish, in which there are eighteen different local boards for the management of the watch, each acting without concert with the other!

The paper marked B contains a list of parishes, in the immediate vicinity of London, in which there is absolutely no watch at all. Think of the state of Brentford and Deptford, with no sort of police by night!

My Bill enables the Secretary of State to abolish gradually the existing watch arrangements, and to substitute in their room a police force that shall act by night and day, under the control of two magistrates. . . . I propose to substitute the new police gradually for the old one, not to attempt too much at first; to begin perhaps with ten or fifteen parishes in the centre of the City of Westminster, and gradually to extend the police district . . .

Letter from Peel to Wellington   *5 November 1829*
I am very glad indeed to hear that you think well of the Police. It has given me from the first to last more trouble than anything I undertook.

I want to teach people that liberty does not consist in having your house robbed by organised gangs of thieves, and in leaving the principal streets of London in the nightly possession of drunken women and vagabonds.

The chief danger of the failure of the new system will be, if it is made a job, if gentlemen's servants and so forth are placed in the higher offices . . .

Sir Robert Peel, ed. C. S. Parker, Vol. II, 1899

4 A cartoon on Peel's new police force, published in 1829

A THUNDERING PEEL TO THIEVES PICKPOCKETS WATCHMEN, &c. &c.

Comment

The increase of poverty and unemployment after 1815 created a real problem of law and order in the new large industrial towns. This was the responsibility of Robert Peel. As home secretary, he made two major contributions — the revision of the criminal code (which considerably reduced the number of capital offences) and the establishment of the Metropolitan Police in 1829. The old system of parish night-watchmen — even though supplemented in some parts by day-time patrols — was hopelessly inefficient and no match for the hardened criminal. Although the 'Peelers' or 'Bobbies' in their black coats and top hats were unpopular at first, the system was quickly copied by other cities.

Questions

a. Draw a small graph to show the increased rate of crime in London between 1822 and 1828.
b. Why was the police system before 1829 so ineffective?
c. Why do you think that Peel decided to change the system *gradually*?
d. What was the main difference between the old watch and the new police?
e. What evidence is there here to suggest that Peel's plans had been opposed?
f. What arguments had clearly been used by those who had opposed him?
g. Examine Plate 4. What did the cartoonist think about Peel's new police force?

19

6 Foreign Policy — Castlereagh and the Congresses

. . . In short, the Grand Assembly of Crowned Heads and Ministers at the ill-starred Congress of Vienna, almost wholly occupied, as they were, in promoting their own aggrandizement, either entirely neglected to take measures for preserving the future tranquillity, or they betrayed the most lamentable ignorance of the public feeling. . . . But civilised nations are not now in a humour to be transferred from sovereign to sovereign like the slaves of Africa. . . . Who is there that thinks the Poles can be satisfied with their country having been rendered a province of Russia? Have they derived any advantage from the downfall of Napoleon? . . .

It was unfortunate for this country that our late Minister for Foreign Affairs had not a sufficient knowledge of the character of the Statesmen of modern Europe. Isolated as the British Cabinet was during so long a period of the war, it was not possible that the English Ministers should have an accurate knowledge of the principles and conduct of the Continental Statesmen.

The honourable character of Lord Londonderry himself tended still further to prevent him from even suspecting that his new friends could act in the manner which he afterwards witnessed with astonishment. And when in addition to these reasons, it is recollected that he suddenly entered into terms of personal intimacy and friendship with these men . . . no one can wonder that he should have been in some respects dazzled and deceived . . .

I have already observed that the Allies had publicly proclaimed the restoration of the *status quo* in Europe, if its different nations assisted them in overthrowing Buonaparte. On the fulfilment of this pledge, the Marquis of Londonderry should have insisted. . . . We formerly traded with the States which were parcelled out at the Congress of Vienna; and if they had been placed on their ancient and independent footing, Great Britain would have immediately resumed her commercial relations with them. But, instead of this . . . the partitioned States are incorporated with Governments who have prohibited or restricted our commerce! . . .

The discerning mind of Mr. Canning will, doubtless draw the true and most useful conclusions from the scene which has passed before him. He is not personally connected with any of the Foreign Courts, nor personally pledged to their measures. The adoption of a new line of policy by him does not carry with it the painful acknowledgment that his former system had been wrong . . .

Lewis Goldsmith, Observations on the Appointment of the Rt. Hon. Geo. Canning, 1822

Comment

The Congress of Vienna, dominated by Austria, Britain, Prussia and Russia, had finally produced a peace settlement in 1815. The victorious allies took suitable rewards for themselves and agreed to hold regular Congresses for the discussion of world problems. Britain's foreign secretary was Viscount Castlereagh, who had played a large part in holding the allies together during the final stages of the war. By the time of his suicide in 1822, however, he had become largely disillusioned by the Congress System. George Canning, his successor, quickly withdrew Britain from membership.

Questions

a. Who were the most 'important' Crowned Heads and Ministers at the Congress of Vienna?

b. What main criticism did Goldsmith make of the discussions at the Congress?

c. Can you think of a more recent example of states being transferred at the end of a war 'from sovereign to sovereign' without any consultation of the inhabitants?

d. Why is this a dangerous policy?

e. Why had Castlereagh been ignorant of the 'character of the statesmen of modern Europe' at the Congress?

f. Give two reasons why Castlereagh was later 'dazzled and deceived' by the other European statesmen.

g. In what way had Castlereagh failed to look after Britain's commercial interests?

h. Why did Goldsmith believe that Canning would make a very much much better foreign secretary?

7 Parliamentary Reform, 1832

The Bath Herald, October 1812
On Wednesday the election for this city came on, when Lord John Thynne and Lieut.-Col. Palmer were re-elected by the Mayor, Aldermen and Common Council.

During the election Mr. Allen appeared in the Hall, and demanded a poll for himself and S. Graves, Esq., insisting upon the right of the Freemen of the City at large to give their suffrages. But they ignored him and carried on chairing the two Members. Mr. Allen, left in the Hall, then took the votes of several Freemen, and after three hours, had got 28 names in support of his pretensions. He adjourned to a neighbouring Inn, from one of the windows of which, he addressed the populace who had collected to an immense number. He invited them to come back the following day.

Macaulay's speech on the Reform Bill, March 1831
. . . I am opposed to Universal Suffrage, because I think it would produce a destructive revolution. I support this plan, because I am sure that it is our best security against a revolution. . . . We say, and we say justly, that it is not by mere numbers, but by property and intelligence, that the nation ought to be governed. Yet, saying this, we exclude from all share in the government great masses of property and intelligence. We do more. We drive over to the side of revolution those whom we shut out from power. Is this a time when the cause of law and order can spare one of its natural allies?

The Weekly Dispatch, January 1833
An analysis of the first reformed Parliament:
BATH: Population 38,063; number of £10 houses 7,314: the old constituency 33.

Bath has hitherto provided one of the most striking illustrations of the anomalies and corrupt absurdities of our constitution. Through a long course of years for ten parliaments, we find Lord John Thynne, brother of the Marquis of Bath, voting against Reform, against Catholic Emancipation, against the Queen, and against every enlightened and patriotic measure.

5 A cartoon on the Reform Movement, 1831

A Radical Reformer. — A Whole Bill Reformer. A bit by bit Reformer. An Anti Reformer.

FOUR SPECIMENS OF THE POLITICAL PUBLICK.

Comment

By 1830 the demand for parliamentary reform was overwhelming. The faults of the old system were plain to see. Middle-class industrialists, deprived of much political say, joined workers, anxious to improve their basic conditions. Strikes and riots added weight to the arguments expressed at reform meetings. The Whigs, back in power under Lord Grey, were mildly sympathetic. Russell's Great Reform Bill, passed at the third attempt in 1832, redistributed many seats to industrial areas and extended the vote in the boroughs to all £10 householders. This gave 652,000 people the franchise, out of a total population of three million adult males in England and Wales.

Questions

a. How were M.P.s elected in Bath before 1832? How many people had the vote?

b. What *percentage* of people had the vote in Bath (i) before, (ii) after the Reform Bill?

c. What evidence is there to suggest that Bath seldom changed its M.P.s?

d. Who were the freemen of the city? How many more people would have voted if Mr. Allen's demand had been met? (See Document 11.)

e. What, in Macaulay's view, should have been the qualifications for voting?

f. Explain why he approved of the Reform Bill.

23

8 The Abolition of Slavery, 1833

There can be no doubt that a great many of the Abolitionists are actuated by very pure motives: they have been shocked at the cruelties which have been and still are very often practised towards slaves, their minds are imbued with the horrors they have read and heard of, and they have an invincible conviction that the state of slavery under any form is repugnant to the spirit of the English Constitution and the Christian religion, and that it is a stain upon the national character which ought to be wiped away. These people, generally speaking, are very ignorant concerning all the various difficulties which beset the questions; their notions are superficial . . .

Talking over the matter the other day, Henry Taylor (of the Colonial Office) said that he was well aware of the consequences of emancipation both to the negroes and the planters. The estates of the latter would not be cultivated; it would be impossible, for want of labour; the negroes would not work — no inducement would be sufficient to make them; they wanted to be free merely that they might be idle. They would, on being emancipated, possess themselves of ground, the fertility of which in those regions is so great that very trifling labour will be sufficient to provide them with the means of existence, and they will thus relapse rapidly into a state of barbarism; they will resume the habits of their African brethren, but, he thinks, without the ferocity and savageness which distinguish the latter. . . . The island would not long be tenable for whites; indeed, it is difficult to conceive how any planters could remain there when their property was no longer cultivable . . .

The Greville Memoirs, Vol. 2, pp. 347–9

Comment

The great anti-slavery campaign, launched earlier by William Wilberforce, had already secured the ban on slave trading in British ships
(1807). Slavery itself continued, however, especially on the plantations
of America and the West Indies. Persistent agitation by Thomas Fowell
Buxton, who had taken over from the ageing Wilberforce, finally led to
the total abolition of slavery within the British Empire in 1833. The Act
freed immediately all slaves under the age of twelve, but compelled the
remainder to stay on for five years as apprentices to their masters.
Compensation was given to plantation owners for the loss of this
'property'.

Questions

a. What reasons did people have for supporting the abolition of
   slavery?
b. What three adjectives (not used in the text) could be used to describe
   the abolitionists?
c. Why did Taylor feel that the Negroes wanted freedom?
d. What would happen to them as a result?
e. How would abolition affect the white population?
f. Explain why slavery was considered to be repugnant to (i) the spirit
   of the English constitution, (ii) the Christian religion.
g. What do you think made Taylor believe that the Negroes would not
   become savages?

9 The Factory Act, 1833

Mr. Abraham Whitehead, called in; and examined.

. . . At how early an age are children employed? — The youngest age at which children are employed is never under five, but some are employed between five and six in woollen mills. How early have you observed these young children going to their work? — In the summertime I have frequently seen them going to work between five and six in the morning. . . . How late in the evening have you seen them to be at work? — I have seen them at work in the summer season between nine and ten in the evening; they continue to work as long as they can see . . .

How do they get their breakfast? — They get their breakfast as they can; they eat and work; there is generally a pot of water porridge, with a little treacle in it, placed at the end of the machine, and when they have exerted themselves to get a little forward with their work, they take a few spoonfuls for a minute or two, and then to work again . . .

Can children employed in this way obtain any instruction from day-schools?—There is no possibility of that; but since this Factory Bill has been agitated, when I have been at mills the children have gathered round me for a minute or two as I passed along, and have said, 'When shall we have to work 10 hours a day? Will you get the Ten Hour Bill? We shall have a rare time then: surely someone will set up a neet [night] school. I will learn to write, that I will . . .'

If protection be afforded by law to children up to the age of 15, do you see any necessity for any further protection? — Those above 15 would then suffer, and why should they continue to work 17 or 18 hours per day? It seems to me that youths ought to have some opportunity of learning to read and write, and other domestic duties . . .

Suppose, from a failure of the profits [as a result of the Bill], that the mill-owners should give up their concerns, would not the result be great distress in the neighbourhood? — If some manufactories gave up . . . it would introduce domestic manufacture, which would be the greatest blessing that could be introduced into Old England; the present factory system is a complete system of slavery and degradation . . .

Report of the Committee on the Factories Bill, 1832

Comment

The employment of children in factories had long been the concern of reformers. Earlier attempts at legislation, however, had met with much opposition. By 1830 a Ten Hour movement had been launched to demand a maximum ten-hour day for all those under the age of twenty-one. The cause was taken up in parliament by Michael Sadler and Lord Ashley. Eventually the government appointed a committee of enquiry and finally passed a Factory Act of its own. This limited work for children under thirteen to nine hours and under eighteen to twelve hours a day. Factory-owners, who were subject to visits from inspectors, were not allowed to employ children under nine years of age.

Questions

a. How many hours a day did young factory children often work in summertime?
b. How did life in the factory endanger the health of these children?
c. What hints are there in this extract that the factory-owners were often hard taskmasters?
d. What opportunities, normally open to children nowadays, were lacking factory children then?
e. Why did Whitehead feel that the Factory Act should apply to young people over fifteen?
f. What suggests that the Ten Hour movement had been well-publicised in the North?
g. Why did mill-owners fear that a Ten Hour Bill would harm their profits? Do you agree with their argument?
h. What was 'domestic manufacture'? Why did many workers prefer that system?

10 The Poor Law Amendment Act, 1834

Mr. James Foard, called in and examined.

You are a member of the board of Guardians at Petworth? — Yes. How long have you been a member of the board? — Ever since the union commenced. Will you state to the Committee generally your impression of what has been the effect of the administration of the New Poor Law at Petworth? — It has been very injurious to men with large families; very oppressive I might have said. In what respects? — I consider that five children and upwards cannot be supported at the price of corn now by a man's earnings of 9s. or 10s. a week. How has it affected other classes? — The other classes perhaps it has not much affected. The aged and infirm? — The aged are taken care of now in their own parish the same as they were before the union. . . . Have you observed the diet in the workhouse? — Yes. Do you consider it a sufficient and wholesome diet? — It is barely sufficient . . .

Edward Pullen, called in and examined.

How many children have you? — Ten. . . . Before the present Poor Law, what was the amount of wages you received: how much a week? — I think it was 10s., I am not certain. What was the greatest weekly allowance that you had from the parish at that time? — I cannot justly say, but somewhere about 4s. or 5s. a week. Then at that time, from wages and parish assistance, you received 15s? — Yes. And all that you are now receiving is 11s. 6d.? — Yes. You state that you have three children in the Union workhouse? — Yes. Are they all boys? — No, two boys and a girl. Have you seen them since they have been there? — Yes, several times. Are the boys separated from the sister? — Yes. In separate apartments? — Yes. Are they kindly treated in this work-house? — I am very well satisfied with them in the workhouse; I know that they are done for better there than I can do for them.

Minutes of the Select Committee on the Poor Law Amendment Act, 1837

6 A cartoon on the Poor Laws, 1836

Comment

The Poor Law Amendment Act attempted to halt the rapid growth in the number of paupers by making poverty unattractive. The old system, which allowed able-bodied men to be given poor relief in their own homes, was thought to encourage idleness at the expense of the parish ratepayers. Under the new system only the sick and aged could receive relief at home. All others would become inmates of the local workhouse, where conditions were made deliberately harsh. In the long term the Act was successful — poverty decreased, wages rose and rates fell. The immediate hardships caused by the Act, however, are illustrated by this extract.

Questions

a. What was Foard's main criticism of the New Poor Law?

b. What effect did it have on the Pullen household?

c. Who was to blame for Pullen's unhappy situation — Pullen, his employer, the parish or the government?

d. What effect did the New Poor Law have on Pullen's *actual* wage (i.e. the money he earned from his employer)? Explain this change.

e. How do these extracts illustrate the deliberate harshness of life in the workhouse?

f. Why, therefore, do you think that Pullen said that he was 'very well satisfied' with the workhouse?

g. Examine Plate 6. What did the cartoonist feel about the poor laws (i) before 1834, (ii) after 1834?

11 The Municipal Corporations Act, 1835

William Clark, Esquire, Mayor of Bath, and Mr. Philip George, Town-Clerk of Bath, called in and examined.

... Have the goodness to describe how that corporation is composed? — It is composed of 10 aldermen and 20 common-councilmen.

How are they chosen? — The members of the corporation, that is, the common-council, are elected out of the free citizens of the city, and the aldermen are elected out of the common-council.

What do you mean by the free citizens? — The freemen of the town who have obtained their freedom by apprenticeship and servitude, or by purchase.

Are they a numerous body? — Altogether about 110; perhaps in that number I include the 30 composing the Corporation ...

How are the 20 common-councilmen elected? — Out of the free citizens.

For life? — For life.

Do the citizens take part in the election of the common-councilmen? — No ...

To whom must a person serve an apprenticeship to become himself, at the expiration of his apprenticeship, a free citizen? — To a free citizen.

Is there any specific time? — Seven years ...

Of course it has been a matter of considerable value to be a member of the corporation of Bath? — I am not aware of that: it gives a man a station in the town certainly.

It gave him considerable power? — No more than any other magistrate would have.

The corporation have, till of late, returned two members to Parliament? — Yes.

Have you perceived that in the Corporation of Bath, as in other cases of close corporations, there was a good deal of relationship between the members of the corporation and those who succeeded? — There are several instances of that.

A kind of hereditary succession? — No, not hereditary certainly, because every member of the Corporation is elected.

They naturally favour their own relations to a considerable extent? — It is possible that may be the case.

Minutes of the Select Committee on Municipal Corporations, 1833

7 A cartoon on
the Corporation
Bill, 1836

WORKING THE CORPORATION BILL

Comment

After the reform of parliament in 1832, it was inevitable that local
government would also be reformed sooner or later. The Municipal
Corporations Act of 1835 ended the old 'closed' type of corporation (of
which Bath was a good example) by granting the vote in local elections
to all ratepayers. Only the chartered boroughs benefited from this at
first, but other towns were allowed to petition for similar privileges.
The Act helped to make councils more efficient and more aware of the
community's needs. Foundations had been laid for the many later
improvements in health and housing.

Questions

a. How were the members of the Bath Corporation elected?
b. What was Bath's population in 1833? (See Document 7.) How many
freemen were there?
c. What two methods enabled a person to become a freeman of the
City?
d. Why was it nevertheless difficult for a person to become a freeman
by these methods?
e. What reasons would a person have (before 1832) for wanting to
become a member of the Corporation?
f. Why were there so few vacancies on the Corporation?
g. Examine Plate 7. Who are the men on the left of the picture? What
do the fat and thin figures represent? Explain the significance of
what is happening.

31

12 The People's Charter, 1838

Mr. T. Attwood said, in rising to present this very extraordinary and important petition. . . . The petition originated in the town of Birmingham . . . and it was now presented to that House with 1,280,000 signatures, the result of not less than 500 meetings, which had been held in support of the principles contained in this petition. At each of those meetings there had been one universal anxious cry of distress — distress, he must say, long disregarded by that House. . . . The men who signed the petition were honest and industrious — of sober and unblemished character — men who had always obeyed the laws. Gentlemen enjoying the wealth handed down to them by hereditary descent, whose wants were provided for by the estates to which they succeeded from their forefathers, could have no idea of the privations suffered by the working men of this country. . . . They had seen no attempt to relieve their sufferings, whether they were hand-loom weavers, artisans, or agricultural labourers. They met with no support or even sympathy, from that House. . . . Although he most cordially supported the petition . . . he washed his hands of any idea of any appeal to physical force; he repudiated all talk of arms — he wished for no arms but the will of the people, legally, fairly, and constitutionally expressed. . . . Having said so much, he should now read the prayer of the petition, which was to the following effect:

'That it might please their honourable House to take the petition into their most serious consideration, and to use their utmost endeavour to pass a law, granting to every man of lawful age, sound mind, and uncontaminated by crime, the right of voting for Members to serve in Parliament; that they would cause a law also to be passed, giving the right to vote by the ballot: that the duration of Parliaments might in no case be of greater duration than one year: that they would abolish all property qualifications, to entitle persons to sit in their honourable House; and that all Members elected to sit in Parliament, should be paid for their services.'

Hansard

Comment

The Chartists' demand for further parliamentary reform was caused by feelings of disappointment in the Reform Bill, anger at the harshness of the New Poor Law and misery at the lack of employment in the 1830s. The 'People's Charter', in the form of a petition, was presented to parliament in 1839 by Thomas Attwood, leader of the Birmingham Political Union. It was rejected — as were the later petitions of 1842 and 1848. The movement, discredited by the violence of some of its members, had collapsed with the coming of better times by 1850. Its ideas were too drastic; its leadership poor; its various groups disunited.

Questions

a. What suggests that the Chartist movement was widespread?
b. What main factor had served to unite the Chartists everywhere?
c. What methods did Attwood favour in forwarding the ideas of the Chartist movement?
d. What suggests that not all Chartists agreed with him over methods?
e. Why was it hard for the gentry to sympathise with the problems of the working class?
f. Why were the handloom weavers suffering hardship at this time?
g. Why did the Chartists demand (i) the secret ballot, (ii) the abolition of property qualifications for M.P.s, (iii) the payment of M.P.s?
h. Which of their demands has still not been made law? Give reasons for this.

8 The Chartist
Movement, 1848.
Part of the procession,
sketched at Blackfriars
Bridge

NOT SO *VERY* UNREASONABLE!!! EH?

9 'John—"My
Mistress says she
hopes you won't call
a meeting of her
Creditors; but if you
will leave your Bill in
the usual way, it
shall be properly
attended to."'
A cartoon
published in 1848

The Chartist Petition, 1848

Comment

In 1848 the Chartists planned to represent their third petition to parliament accompanied by a large procession. Although the government refused to allow this to enter the City, the petition itself was eventually delivered by Feargus O'Connor who claimed a total of six million signatures. It was later discovered that in reality under two million people had signed.

Questions

a. Examine Plate 8, which is a sketch made at the time.
   (i) How well was the demonstration organised?
   (ii) Is there any evidence of police supervision?
b. Examine Plate 9, which is a *Punch* cartoon.
   (i) How does it suggest that the Charter's demands were reasonable?
   (ii) Who is 'John' (the figure on the right)? Who is his 'mistress' and 'her creditors'? (See the caption.)

13 Sir Robert Peel

No one speaks well of him; he is even charged with not having a friend. Curses have been hurled at him by his party, which would have withered a weaker moral nature. The Tories fear him; the Whigs hate him; the Chartists affect to despise him. Those who look back, and regret the past, accuse him of treachery. Those who look forward and contemplate the future . . . say he is governing without a principle of government. . . . As he enters at the green door below the bar, and the members, of whatever party, instinctively make way for him, he looks at no one, recognizes no one, receives salutation from no one. . . . Arrived at his place, he exchanges no recognitions with his immediate colleagues, but sits apart, — his body prone upon his crossed legs, his hat down upon his ears, his face stretched forward in anxious attention . . .

He does rule; but as no man ever ruled yet in the Commons House of Parliament. . . . He is not beloved, esteemed, followed with admiration. His power is solitary, self-created. He sees in the House an aggregate meeting of rival interests. In their mutual jealousy, and consequent weakness, lies his power. He holds the balance . . .

As a statesman, Sir Robert Peel seems to identify himself with the middle classes. . . . He is himself a sort of representative of those classes. His loose, long frock coat, odd, cylindrical, small-rimmed hat and drab nether garments, while quite in keeping with the man, are anything but in character with the garb of an aristocrat. . . . Reluctantly followed by the aristocracy, he seems too deeply to know he is not one of the order . . .

If Sir Robert Peel stands alone, it is from choice. He can the better work out his views. He has known the fetters of party friendship, the virulence of its hatred. . . . For, this statesman, so abused, so charged with mediocrity, weakness, insincerity, has really a strong character and fixed purposes. Read his speech on moving the Emancipation Bill . . . you will find proof enough that there is a strong undercurrent of deep feeling and moral energy . . .

Since 1840 his public life has been a series of progressive developments. He began by laying down the principle, that his duty to the public was superior to any obligations to his party. He recognised the nation as his only master. . . . He may be hated, despised, undervalued: but he is wanted.

Sir Robert Peel — Statesman and Orator, 1846

Comment

By the time of his second ministry (1841–46), Peel had already had considerable experience of political life. Entering parliament in 1809, he became chief secretary for Ireland (1812–18) and home secretary (1822–27 under Liverpool, and was then appointed leader of the house under Wellington (1828–30)). Peel's brilliant mind, trained at Harrow and Oxford, gave him a ready grasp of the economic problems of the day; his industrial background, provided by his father's cotton factories, furnished him with an understanding of the needs of the middle class. Although, by nature, he was hardworking and efficient, he was also rather cold and aloof.

Questions

a. What evidence is there to suggest that Peel was a lonely figure?
b. Why did he prefer this form of existence?
c. Which people would 'look back' and 'accuse him of treachery'? Why?
d. What were the other main criticisms made of Peel?
e. Why, in spite of his unpopularity, was Peel able to keep himself in power?
f. Is there anything to suggest that Peel was a man of courage and strong principles?
g. What main groups formed the basis of Peel's party? What reasons would they each have for joining? (See Document 14.)
h. What attitude did Peel have to his party? (See also Document 18.)

14 The New Conservative Party, 1834

To the Electors of the Borough of Tamworth.

GENTLEMEN, . . . I feel it incumbent upon me to enter into a declaration of my views of public policy. . . . I will never admit that I have been, either before or after the Reform Bill, the defender of abuses, or the enemy of judicious reforms. I appeal with confidence, in denial of the charge, to the active part I took in the great question of the Currency — in the consolidation and amendment of the Criminal Law — in the revisal of the whole system of Trial by Jury . . .

With respect to the Reform Bill itself, I will repeat now the declaration which I made when I entered the House of Commons as a Member of the Reformed Parliament, that I consider the Reform Bill a final and irrevocable settlement of a great Constitutional question — a settlement which no friend to the peace and welfare of this country would attempt to disturb, either by direct or insidious means.

Then, as to the spirit of the Reform Bill, and the willingness to adopt and enforce it as a rule of government; if, by adopting the spirit of the Reform Bill, it be meant that we are to live in a perpetual whirlwind of agitation; that public men can only support themselves in public estimation by adopting every impression of the day — by promising the instant redress of anything which anybody may call an abuse . . . if this be the spirit of the Reform Bill, I will not undertake to adopt it. But if the spirit of the Reform Bill implies merely a careful review of institutions, civil and ecclesiastical, undertaken in a friendly temper, combining, with the firm maintenance of established rights, the correction of proved abuses and the redress of real grievances — in that case, I can for myself and colleagues undertake to act in such a spirit and with such intentions.

The Tamworth Manifesto, 1834

Comment

Although Peel had advocated a number of important reforms during the 1820s (see Documents 4 and 5), he had nevertheless been a firm opponent of Parliamentary Reform in 1832. When, however, Peel was invited by William IV to form a government in 1834, he took the opportunity to restate his views in a letter addressed to his own constituency at Tamworth. This 'Tamworth Manifesto' outlined the new *Conservative* policy, as opposed to the old *Tory* policy of men like Liverpool and Wellington. Although his first ministry only lasted a few months, the years between 1835 and 1841 were spent in building up this new Conservative party.

Questions

a. What was Peel's attitude to the Reform Bill by 1835?
b. When had he first announced his changed views?
c. Why had he taken up this new position?
d. What had been Peel's attitude to other reforms during the early part of his career? (See also Documents 4 and 5.)
e. What did Peel fear might happen as a result of the success of the Reform Bill?
f. What *was* Peel prepared to reform in the future?
g. What conditions did he lay down as the basis for any such reform?
h. In what way does the Tamworth Manifesto illustrate the difference in policy between the old Tory party and the new Conservative party? (See also Document 2.)

15 Income Tax, 1842

In the year 1798, when the prospects of this country were most gloomy, the minister had the courage to propose, and the people had the fortitude to adopt, an income tax to the amount of ten per cent. I propose that the duty imposed on incomes should not exceed three per cent., and should, in point of fact, amount to £2. 18s. 4d. per cent. In 1814 incomes of £60 were exempted from taxation, and those from £60 to £150 were taxed at a reduced rate. I shall propose, that from this income tax all incomes under £150 should be exempted . . .

11 March 1842

Why did we propose it? Why did we call upon the country to submit to a tax so unpopular and obnoxious? and why did the country respond to the call? Because they acknowledged . . . that you, the late government, having alienated France, having done nothing to improve our relations or adjust our differences with the United States, had undertaken three wars at a great distance from your resources — war in Syria, war with China, war in Afghanistan; that you had at the same time contrived to make your annual revenue fall short of your expenditure by £2,500,000. . . . These facts sank deep into the public mind, and resistance to income tax was hopeless.

10 August 1842

One of my reasons for proposing the income tax, is, that I might be able to effect the reductions contemplated by the tariff. It includes a sacrifice of revenue to the extent of £1,200,000 . . .

25 April 1842

. . . I have no doubt that a large revenue might have been derived from a duty on beer. But I do say, that I consider it more just and more prudent to meet the difficulty at once by proposing a tax upon incomes, than by reviving indirect taxes, which entail a heavy expense in collecting, and which cannot be reinforced without greatly disturbing the trade and manufactures of the country. I solve the difficulty by the income tax at the same time that I relieve the consumer by reducing the taxation upon articles of general consumption.

23 March 1842
W. T. Haly, *The Opinions of Sir Robert Peel*

Comment

When Peel became prime minister in 1841, the country's finances were in a sorry state. For several years the Whigs had failed to balance the budget. Peel, who was anxious to encourage British trade and industry, avoided the temptation to increase customs duties and indirect taxes. Instead, he brought back the income tax, which had previously been imposed between 1798 and 1816 during the French Wars. The extra revenue raised in this way enabled him not only to balance his budgets, but also to reduce considerably the number of customs duties. Real progress had thus been made in bringing about free trade. Peel's financial reforms — including the Bank Charter Act (1844), which restricted the issue of bank notes — helped to produce Britain's prosperity during the second half of the century.

Questions

a. Which prime minister had imposed the income tax in 1798?
b. In what ways did Peel's income tax differ from that of 1798? How much tax would be payable in each pound?
c. What two main reasons did Peel give for reintroducing the income tax?
d. Why did Peel consider that the income tax was (i) more just; (ii) more prudent than indirect taxes?
e. How would (i) the poorer workers; (ii) smugglers be affected by these proposals?
f. How does this extract illustrate the suggestion that 'Peel seems to identify himself with the middle classes'? (See Document 13.)
g. In what way had the 'late government' alienated France?
h. What were the reasons for the wars in Syria, China and Afghanistan?

16 The Mines Act, 1842

The evidence of Mr. Wild, Chief Constable of Oldham:
There have been a deal of accidents to children and young persons as well as to men, in the mines here, during the last five or six years. But there is a class of accidents of which children employed at coal-works in this neighbourhood are the cause to persons of all ages. These occur in the winding up by the steam-machinery of all persons out of the pit. It is a general system here to employ mere children to tend these engines, and to stop them at the proper moment, and if they be not stopped, the two or three or four or five persons wound up together are thrown over the beam down into the pit again. The inducement to employ these children in circumstances where life and death depend on their momentary attention, is merely that their services can be obtained for perhaps 5s. or 7s. a week instead of the 30s. a week which the proprietors would perhaps have to pay a man of full years and discretion. . . . Three or four boys were killed in this way at the Chamberlane Colliery of Messrs Jones, two or three years since, by the momentary neglect of a little boy, whom he thinks was only nine years of age, and who he heard had turned away from the engine when it was winding up, on his attention being distracted by a mouse in the hearth.

David Hynde, nine years old, coal-putter and hewer: Began to work in the bowels of the earth nine months since at this place; was taken down by father and mother, who work below, and so does sister.

William Burnside, ten years old, coal-bearer: I gang with brother and sister. I can fill one tub in the day: it takes me 17 journeys as my back gets sore. A tub holds near 5 cwt, I follow sister with bits of coal strapped over my head and back.

Margaret Hipps, seventeen years old, putter: My employment, after reaching the wall-face, is to fill a bagie or slype, with $2\frac{1}{2}$ to 3 cwt of coal. I then hook it onto my chain, and drag it through the seam, which is 26 to 28 inches high, till I get to the main-road — a good distance, probably 200 to 400 yards. The pavement I drag over is wet and I am obliged at all times to crawl on hands and feet.

Report of Commissioners on Children's Employment, 1842

Comment

In 1840, thanks to the agitation of Lord Ashley, a committee was set up to investigate working conditions in the mines. Its report, published two years later, described vividly the arduous and dangerous tasks undertaken by women and young children. Although Peel was not personally enthusiastic about reform at this stage, he did allow Ashley to promote the Mines Act of 1842. By this all women and boys under ten were forbidden to work underground. Inspectors were also to see that no child under fifteen was left in charge of winding machinery at the pit head. These extracts are taken from the report. A 'Slype' was a wooden box on sledge-like iron runners. A 'putter' was responsible for dragging or pushing carts of coal.

Questions

a. How were miners carried up to the top of the shafts?
b. Why were children employed to operate the winding gear?
c. What exactly did the child have to do with the machinery?
d. What exactly happened if the child failed to do his job?
e. What other jobs were children expected to undertake in mines?
f. What two different methods of transporting coal are illustrated by these extracts?
g. What effects do you think working in the mines would have on
   (i) the health, (ii) the home life of these children?
h. How would the various people mentioned here be affected by the Mines Act of 1842? Would they welcome the changes?

10 Labour conditions for children in the 1840s

11 Woman and child working in a coalmine

44

Life in Factories and Mines, 1840

Comment

These contemporary drawings illustrate conditions of work for children and women in factories and mines. (See also Documents 9 and 16.)

Questions

a. Examine Plate 10.
  (i) What sort of factory is shown here? Who are the men in the background?
  (ii) Why do you think the people in the foreground are so miserable? Is any of the work dangerous?
b. Examine Plate 11 (which is one of the illustrations used by Ashley in his report on the mines).
  (i) Describe in your own words how the coal was transported along the shaft.
  (ii) In what ways was this work both dangerous and unhealthy?

17 The Maynooth Grant, 1843

The most serious fact of all connected with the present agitation has yet to be mentioned. There cannot be a doubt that the great body of the Roman Catholic priests have gone into the movement in the worst, that is, in the rebellious sense. Many of the priests of the old school, who had been educated in France, and had seen the world, held out for a time; . . . but the curates and young priests brought up at Maynooth have gone into it heartily, almost to a man. These young men are generally the sons of small farmers, and other persons of a similar rank in life. They, therefore, bring with them strong feelings and limited and one-sided information from home; and at Maynooth they are brought up to regard the Church as the sole object for which they are to live, and think, and act. They have no property, no families of their own, to be compromised by a rebellion. . . . They may gain, but they cannot well lose, by the result of a conflict. Some, more heady and enthusiastic than the rest, might even lead their flocks to battle. . . . The priests have given to the repeal movement all the weight of a religious cause in the eyes of a superstitious people.

The Morning Chronicle, October 1843

Do you, in your bill, propose to correct this? to abate the evil? You propose to increase it, to aggravate it, to lengthen the period, to increase the intensity of bigotted education. The students under this system are already too numerous; we increase them. They already stay there too long for any liberal education: we shall enable them to stay longer. They have, and this is your complaint, only £22 per annum; and only a portion of them have that sum. We raise the bursary to £28 and we extend it to the whole five hundred. In the name of common sense, was there ever such a proposal! . . . The result of your system must be to attract to the College the very dregs of the people, and to deter from it every man of better education and more liberal mind.

J. C. Colquhoun's Speech in the Commons, 11 April 1843

Comment

Peel had never been able to escape very far from the Irish problem. As chief secretary for Ireland (1812–18) he had been able to study the difficulties at first hand. Then in 1828 he had agreed reluctantly with Wellington that Catholic Emancipation should be granted in order to prevent an Irish rebellion. (See Document 4.) By 1842 Daniel O'Connell had launched another campaign — this time for the repeal of the Act of Union, by which Ireland was governed from Westminster. Peel dealt firmly with the ensuing demonstrations, but showed his anxiety to help the Irish by improving their facilities for higher education. Three new colleges were set up at Queen's University, while the annual grant to Maynooth College — a training centre for Catholic priests — was increased from £9,000 to £26,000. The latter provoked an angry storm of opposition.

Questions

a. What influence did home background have on the young priests of Maynooth College?
b. What effect did the teaching at Maynooth have on them?
c. Why were they not worried by the prospect of a rebellion?
d. Why were the older priests less revolutionary than those from Maynooth?
e. What exactly were the aims of 'the repeal movement'?
f. How had the priests contributed to this movement?
g. Why was Colquhoun so opposed to the government's proposal to give more money to Maynooth College?
h. From the tone of these extracts, what *sort* of people, do you think, opposed the government on this question?

18 The Repeal of the Corn Laws, 1846

The reports of the potato crop are bad today — this I heard at Abraham's seed shop, who had his information from various quarters. My impression is that three months hence the potatoes will be nearly if not quite gone. I hope I may be mistaken. By the 1st of next month we shall know to a tolerable certainty whether they are gradually rotting in the pits; if they are, they will be all useless by February. I think Government should make up its mind what to do, and to be prepared for what must be done when the calamity is approaching our doors; let it once knock at them, and in the present frame of mind of the people I will not answer for the consequences.

The farmers, with a good crop of corn and high prices, will struggle through the year; but what will you do with the unemployed multitude, whose store of provisions for the next ten months is gone, and who have not a shilling to purchase food?

Lord Clare to the Government, 5 November 1845

An abandonment of your former opinions now would, I think, prejudice your and our characters as public men. . . . I fairly own that I do not see how the repeal of the Corn Law is to afford relief to the distress with which we are threatened. . . . I think it next to impossible to show that the abandonment of the law now could materially affect this year's supply. . . . When the public feel, as I believe they do, great doubts as to the existence of an adequate necessity — they will, I fear, tax us, with treachery and deception . . .

So much as to the effect on our character as public men. But I view with greater alarm its effects on public interests. In my opinion, the party of which you are the head is the only barrier which remains against the revolutionary effects of the Reform Bill. So long as that party remains unbroken, it has the means of doing much good, or at least of preventing much evil. But if it be broken in pieces by a destruction of confidence in its leaders (and I cannot but think that an abandonment of the Corn Law would produce that result), I see nothing before us but the exasperation of class animosities, a struggle for pre-eminence, and the ultimate triumph of unrestrained democracy.

Mr. Goulburn's letter to Peel, 30 November 1845

12 A cartoon of Sir Robert Peel

PEEL'S CHEAP BREAD SHOP.

Comment

The Corn Laws of 1815 had been passed to safeguard the interests of British farmers against the threat of cheap foreign corn. (See Document 1.) In 1839, however, the Anti-Corn Law League had been established by Richard Cobden and John Bright, with the support of many industrialists. Peel, the son of a factory-owner, sympathised with their views but, as the leader of a party which contained many landowners, found it difficult to act. But in 1845 the vast majority of Irish workers, who relied almost entirely on the potato for existence, were suddenly flung into a state of starvation by the failure of their blight-infested crop. There was no prospect of relief supplies from England, where corn was scarce and costly. Under these alarming circumstances Peel decided to end the restrictions on imported grain. The repeal of the Corn Laws in 1846 split asunder the Conservative party.

Questions

a. What evidence is there here that the Irish worker (i) regarded the potato as his main item of food, (ii) grew his own supply for the year, (iii) was desperately poor?
b. Why was Mr. Abraham concerned about the potato crop?
c. Why were the farmers not so desperate?
d. What 'calamity' does Lord Clare obviously fear?

19 Lord Palmerston

I do not hesitate to say that the two great objects of his heart — one, the
institution of a true and vigorous foreign policy, suited to the honour
and position of the Kingdom of England; the other the extinction of the
slave trade — were founded, not only on his personal love of freedom
(which was intense), but on his deep and unalterable conviction that
civil liberty all over the world would be good for the human race.

His ardour to abolish the traffic in slaves was stimulated constantly
by the atrocities of the system, for he could feel very keenly the wrongs
of others. And though, doubtless, many will criticise him unsparingly
for his efforts at constitutions in foreign countries, he would reply that
representative government, with all its abuses, is the best for the safety,
honour and improvement of mankind; and that he would never flinch
from any legitimate opportunity to urge its advancement.

Such vigorous assertion of his own principles, in the face of very
hostile and sensitive powers, was often misconstrued as a readiness for
war. . . . From war, as war, I believe he shrank with horror; but he was
inflexibly of the opinion that the best way to avoid it was to speak out
boldly, and ever be prepared to meet the emergency . . .

Unquestionably he was born for a bureau; the thing and its whole
surroundings were part of his existence. It amounted to a complete
absorbtion of the man in his devotion to the special duties. . . . On
matters where he fully believed that he was master of the subject his
conclusions were very decided and positively unchangeable; and yet
no one will say that, either in public debate or private conversation, he
maintained his opinions offensively . . .

The testimony that I bear is, perhaps, of little value, as being that of a
man who had ever received from him the look, the voice and the action
of kindness. But take the testimony of Sir R. Peel, a political antagonist:
'We may have many differences of opinion with the noble lord, but the
country is proud of him'.

Letter from Lord Shaftesbury to the Hon. E. Ashley, 1876

13 A cartoon of Palmerston

LORD PALMERSTON'S UNPOPULAR EXHIBITION.

Comment

Although Palmerston had held the office of secretary-at-war under the Tories (1809–28), he was a Liberal at heart. It was therefore no surprise when Lord Grey invited him to become foreign secretary of the Whig government in 1830 — a position he held until 1851 (apart from the years of Peel's administration). Then, having served as home secretary from 1852 to 1855, he became prime minister with one short break — until the time of his death in 1865. During these years he became one of the most popular characters in Britain and one of the most hated statesmen abroad. Courageous in action, his confidence was founded largely on the wealth of England's industry and the power of its navy.

Questions

a. How does this extract illustrate the qualities of Palmerston (i) as a person, (ii) as a foreign secretary?
b. How does this extract illustrate (i) the aims, (ii) the methods of his foreign policy?
c. Which powers in particular were 'very hostile and sensitive' to Palmerston's policy? Why?
d. What criticisms were made of Palmerston's policy in England? Why?
e. Why did Palmerston dislike the slave trade?
f. Why did Palmerston try so often to set up 'constitutions' in other countries? Give examples of this policy.

20 The Quadruple Alliance, 1834

I have been very busy ever since I returned from Broadlands on the 4th of this month, working out my quadruple alliance between England, France, Spain and Portugal, for the expulsion of Carlos and Miguel from the Portuguese dominions, and I hope it will be signed tomorrow. I carried it through the Cabinet by a *coup de main*, taking them by surprise, and not leaving them time to make objections. . . . I reckon this to be a great stroke. In the first place it will settle Portugal, and go some way to settle Spain also. But, what is of more permanent and extensive importance, it establishes a quadruple alliance among the constitutional states of the west, which will serve as a powerful counterpoise to the Holy Alliance of the east. I have, ever since Ferdinand's death, felt that morally this alliance must exist; but it was not till a fortnight ago that I saw the opportunity of giving it a substantive and practical form. The renewal of the Spanish wish that we should send troops to Portugal, suggested the idea to me. . . . Those who will like it least, after the two Infants, are Pedro and his ministers, who wish the Civil War to go on, that they may continue to plunder and confiscate. . . . I should like to see Metternich's face when he reads our treaty . . .

With Russia we are just as we were, snarling at each other, hating each other, but neither wishing for war. Their last communication on Eastern affairs is anything but satisfactory. However, there is no danger of anything being done by them. They cannot return to Turkey unless invited by the Sultan, and the Sultan will not invite them unless attacked by Mehemet Ali; but Mehemet Ali will not stir as long as we beg him not to do so, because he knows that our fleet could effectually prevent him. He cannot carry on war in Asia Minor without communication by sea with Egypt, and that we could effectually cut off.

Palmerston's letter to his brother, 21 April 1834

Comment

Palmerston's great dislike of absolute rulers led him, wherever possible, to encourage the setting up of constitutional monarchies on the British pattern. In 1834, therefore, he seized the opportunity to support the young liberal governments in Spain and Portugal by forming a Quadruple Alliance (with France as the other member). King Ferdinand's bequest of the Spanish crown to his infant daughter Isabella was being challenged by her absolutist brother, Don Carlos. In Portugal the liberal Don Pedro had succeeded in putting his daughter, Donna Maria, on the throne, thus displacing another absolutist, Don Miguel. Palmerston sent forces to suppress the supporters of Don Carlos and Don Miguel and to prevent any help being sent to them by Russia, Prussia or Austria.

Questions

a. What was the main difference between the states in the Quadruple Alliance and those in the Holy Alliance?

b. What was the *immediate* aim of the Quadruple Alliance?

c. Why did Palmerston feel that the alliance would also be important in the long term?

d. Which individuals would most regret the success of the Quadruple Alliance? Why?

e. What does this extract tell us about Palmerston's qualities as a statesman?

f. Why were Britain and Russia 'snarling at each other' so much at this time? In what ways did their interests clash?

g. What conditions were needed before Russia could again move its troops into Turkey?

h. Why was Palmerston so confident that these conditions would not arise?

21 The Eastern Question, 1839–41

The particular and immediate object which I have been endeavouring for some months past to accomplish, in conjunction with the representatives of Austria, Russia and Prussia, has been to persuade the French Government to come in to some plan of arrangement between the Sultan and Mehemet Ali. . . . The question which the British Government now has to decide is, whether the four Powers, having failed in persuading France to join them, will or will not proceed to accomplish their purpose without the assistance of France . . .

My opinion upon this question is distinct and unqualified. I think that the object to be attained is of the utmost importance for the interests of England, for the preservation of the balance of power, and for the maintenance of peace in Europe; . . . I think that if we draw back, and shrink from a co-operation with Austria, Russia and Prussia in this matter, because France stands aloof and will not join, we shall . . . virtually acknowledge that we dare embark in no system of policy in opposition to the will of France. Now this appears to be to be a principle of policy which is not suitable to the power and station of England . . .

The immediate result of our declining to go on with the three Powers because France does not join us will be, that Russia will withdraw her offers to unite herself with the other Powers for a settlement of the affairs of Turkey, and she will again resume her separate and isolated position with respect to those affairs; and you will have the Treaty of Unkiar Skelessi renewed under some still more objectionable form . . .

The ultimate results of such a decision will be the practical division of the Turkish empire into two separate and independent States, whereof one will be a dependency of France, and the other a satellite of Russia; and in both of which our political influence will be annulled, and our commercial interests will be sacrificed; and this dismembermenty will inevitably give rise to local struggles and conflicts which will involve the Powers of Europe in most serious disputes.

Palmerston's letter to Melbourne, 5 July 1840

Comment

In 1833 Mehemet Ali of Egypt rebelled against his overlord, the sultan of Turkey, and swept rapidly with his forces towards Constantinople. The sultan, in this hour of crisis, turned to Russian troops to save him from disaster. Russia was duly rewarded in the Treaty of Unkiar Skelessi with the sole right of sailing warships through the Dardanelles Straits. Palmerston was alarmed at Russia's growing influence over Turkey and the obvious threat to Britain's control of the Mediterranean. When, therefore, Mehemet Ali again attacked Turkey in 1839, Palmerston insisted that the great Powers should intervene jointly. Although France — an ally of Egypt — refused to co-operate, Mehemet Ali was eventually defeated. Palmerston successfully removed Russia's previous gains in the Dardanelles Convention of 1841.

Questions

a. Why do you think Palmerston was so anxious to persuade the French to take joint action in the Middle East with the other powers? Why did the French refuse to join?

b. What was the immediate aim of the proposed intervention by the powers?

c. Why was this crisis in the Middle East of such importance (i) for the interest of England, (ii) for the preservation of the balance of power, (iii) for the maintenance of the peace in Europe?

d. What did Palmerston fear would happen if both France and Britain failed to co-operate with the other powers?

e. What other reasons did Palmerston give for believing that Britain should proceed in this matter *without* France if necessary?

f. According to Palmerston, what effects would the breakdown of joint negotiations have (i) on the Turkish Empire, (ii) the fortunes of Russia, France and Britain?

g. When was the Turkish Empire finally partitioned? Was Palmerston right in his prophecy that it would give rise to local struggles?

22 The Don Pacifico Affair, 1849–50

I have desired the Admiralty to instruct Sir William Parker to take Athens on his way back from the Dardanelles, and to support you in bringing at last to a satisfactory ending the settlement of our various claims upon the Greek Government. You will of course, in conjunction with him, persevere in the negotiations as long as is consistent with our dignity and honour, and I measure that time by days. If, however, the Greek Government does not strike, Parker must do so. In that case you should embark on board his fleet before he begins to take any hostile steps, in order that you and your mission may be secure against insult. He should, of course, begin by reprisals; that is by taking possession of some Greek property. . . . The next thing would be a blockade of any or all of his ports. . . . Of course Pacifico's claim must be fully satisfied.

Palmerston's letter to Wyse, the minister in Athens, December 1849

We do not mind the Russian swagger and attempt to bully about Greece. We shall pursue our own course steadily and firmly, and we must and shall obtain the satisfaction we require. . . . They are furious at seeing that the spoilt child of Absolutism, whom they have been encouraging on for many years past to insult and defy England, should at last have received a punishment from which they are unable to protect him. . . . As to Nesselrodes mysterious hints of evil consequences which may follow if we continue to detain the Greek merchant ships, he may be assured that we shall detain them till we get paid . . .

Palmerston's letter to Bloomfield, the minister in St. Petersburg, March 1850

I, therefore, fearlessly challenge the verdict which this House is to give on the question now brought before it . . . whether, as the Roman in days of old held himself free from indignity when he could say, 'Civus Romanus sum', so also a British subject, in whatever land he may be, shall feel confident that the watchful eye on the strong arm of England will protect him against injustice and wrong.

Palmerston's speech to the Commons, June 1850

Comment

The Don Pacifico affair best illustrates Palmerston's intense patriotism and his high-handed methods of bullying offending countries into submission. He detested the corrupt and despotic Greek government of King Otho; he disliked the influence which Russia, Prussia and Austria exerted there; he resented the ruler's bad faith in paying debts. When, therefore, Don Pacifico — a British subject — appealed to him for help, he responded promptly and with vigour. Don Pacifico's house had been ransacked and gutted by a mob during local riots. For three years his claim for compensation had been rejected. Palmerston won the case by giving it the backing of a British fleet!

Questions

a. How do these extracts illustrate Palmerston's absolute determination to gain compensation from the Greek government?
b. What immediate action was Parker ordered to take?
c. What action had he in fact taken by March 1850?
d. What evidence is there to suggest that Britain had had trouble with Greece for some years?
e. Why was Palmerston so confident of success and so unconcerned about Russia's threats?
f. Why were the Russians so interested in Greece?
g. How did Palmerston justify this intervention? Do you feel that he was right?
h. Would intervention of this kind be possible today? How do governments seek to protect their subjects in foreign countries?

23 Palmerston's Dismissal, 1851

The Queen requires, first, that Lord Palmerston will distinctly state what he proposes in a given case, in order that the Queen may know as distinctly to what she is giving her royal sanction.

Secondly, having once given her sanction to a measure, that it be not arbitrarily altered or modified by the minister. Such an act she must consider as failing in sincerity towards the Crown, and justly to be visited by the exercise of her constitutional right of dismissing that minister. She expects to be kept informed of what passes between him and the foreign ministers before important decisions are taken based upon that intercourse; to receive the foreign despatches in good time, and to have the drafts for her approval sent to her in sufficient time to make herself acquainted with their contents before they must be sent off.

The Queen's letter to Lord John Russell, August 1850

The history of my dismissal is short and simple. I had, like all the rest of the world, long considered the French Constitution of 1848 as one that would not long work, and as an arrangement which approached to the very verge of anarchy. The course pursued by the Assembly showed that a conflict between that body and the President was inevitable; and it seemed to me better that in such a conflict the President should prevail over the Assembly. Therefore, when the *coup d'état* took place, and Walewsky came to me on the Tuesday to tell me of it. I expressed to him these opinions. . . . John Russell replied that I mistook the point at issue between us. The question was not whether the President was or was not justified in doing what he has done, but whether I was justified in expressing any opinion thereupon to Walewsky without having first taken the opinion of the Cabinet on that matter. . . . My letter left him no alternative but to advise the Queen to place the Foreign Office in other hands.

Palmerston's letter to his brother, 22 January 1852

Comment

Both Queen Victoria and her husband, Prince Albert, were deeply interested in foreign affairs. They were, therefore, extremely irritated by Palmerston's frequent failure to consult either the cabinet or the crown and by his tendency to support rebellious subjects against despotic rulers. Palmerston's great self-confidence often caused him to act on his own initiative. Consequently, in an unguarded moment, he welcomed the news of Louis Napoleon's *coup d'état*, brought to him by the French ambassador (1851). This was taken in France as the official approval of the British government — much to the anger of the queen and the prime minister, Lord John Russell. The cabinet, in fact, had only just agreed that it should remain neutral for the present towards the changes in France.

Questions

a. What exact information did the queen require from the foreign secretary?

b. What evidence is there to suggest that the queen intended to express her own views on foreign affairs?

c. What behaviour in particular had caused the queen to threaten Palmerston's dismissal in 1850?

d. Why had Palmerston been in favour of Napoleon's *coup d'état*?

e. Why did Russell dismiss Palmerston from the government?

f. What do we learn about Palmerston himself from these passages?

g. How do these extracts illustrate the various powers and responsibilities of (i) the monarch, (ii) the prime minister, (iii) the cabinet, (iv) individual ministers under British constitution?

24 The Siege of Sebastopol, 1855

Dr. Hall to Lord Raglan, 2 March 1855

This afternoon 100 patients were to be removed from the General Hospital at Balaklava to the Convalescent Establishment on the plateau of the old castle, overlooking the sea. . . . The road up to the huts could easily be made practicable for ambulance mules. The position of the huts I think promises every advantage; they are placed on a dry ridge overlooking the sea, sufficiently removed from the noise and stench of the town, and not too far from our stores and resources . . .

Bowel complaints continue to be the most prevalent class of diseases; but I think they are not so serious as they were a short time ago, nor is scurvy so manifest as it was since the issue of lime juice daily as a portion of the men's rations. . . . If the issue of fresh meat could be insured, together with vegetables and lime juice, I am quite satisfied, now that the men are warmly clad, and will soon be better sheltered, a manifest improvement would take place in their health.

Lord Raglan to Lord Panmure. Before Sebastopol, 19 June 1855

The flank columns at once obeyed the signal to advance, preceded by covering parties of the Rifle Brigade, and by sailors carrying ladders and soldiers carrying wool-bags; but they had no sooner shown themselves beyond the trenches than they were assailed by a most murderous fire of grape and musketry. Those in advance were either killed or wounded, and the remainder found it impossible to proceed. I never before witnessed such a continued and heavy fire of grape combined with musketry from the enemy's works, which appeared to be fully manned; and the long list of killed and wounded will show that a very large proportion of those that went forward fell . . .

The superiority of our fire on the day we opened, led both General Pelissier and myself to conclude that the Russian Artillery fire was, in a great measure subdued. The result has shown that the resources of the enemy were not exhausted, and that they still had the power to bring an overwhelming fire upon their assailants.

Capt. Sayer (ed.), *Despatches and Papers*

14 The New Castle Hospital at Balaclava

15 The capture of the Malakoff Tower, Sebastopol

Comment

Nicholas I's claim to protect all Greek Orthodox members of the Turkish Empire was seen by Palmerston as yet another attempt by Russia to expand into the Mediterranean. (See Document 21.) When, therefore, Russia invaded Moldavia and Wallachia in 1853, France and Britain — with strong support from public opinion — declared war. A joint force under Lord Raglan landed in the Crimea (September 1854) with the object of capturing the fortress of Sebastopol. The Russian defences proved too strong, the weather too wretched and the supplies too unreliable. Before Sebastopol fell (September 1855) and the Treaty of Paris brought the war to an end (March 1856), thousands had died of disease and enemy bullets.

Questions

a. Why was the General Hospital not very suitable for convalescence?
b. Why did Dr. Hall feel that the new site was so good? (See also Plate 14.)
c. What conditions had contributed to the poor state of health in the army?
d. What changes had caused some improvement to take place?
e. Why did some men carry ladders and wool-bags during the attack on Sebastopol? (See also Plate 15.)
f. What had prompted the allied attack to take place?
g. How does this extract illustrate the methods of warfare at this time? (See also Plate 15.)

25 Gladstone

This man was a wonderful being, physically and mentally, the mental part being well sustained by the physical. His eye was intensely bright, though in the rest of the face there was nothing especially indicative of genius. His physical and mental force was such that he could speak for more than four hours at a stretch, and with vigour and freshness so sustained that George Venables, a not over-friendly critic, after hearing him for four hours, and on a financial subject, wished that he could go on for four hours more. His powers of work were enormous. He once called me to him to help in settling the details of a University Bill. He told me that he had been up over the Bill late at night. We worked at it together from ten in the morning till six in the afternoon, saving an hour and a half which he spent at Privy Council, leaving me with the Bill. When we parted he went down to the House, where he spoke at one o'clock the next morning. Besides his mountain of business, he was a voluminous writer on other than political subjects, and did a vast amount of miscellaneous reading . . .

Like Pitt, Gladstone was a first-rate sleeper . . . [Mrs. Gladstone said] that he would come home from the most exciting debate and fall at once into sound sleep. . . . In extreme old age he took long walks and felled trees, conversed with unfailing vivacity, and seemed to be the last of the party in the evening to wish to go to bed . . .

To me, Gladstone's life is specially interesting as that of a man who was a fearless and powerful upholder of humanity and righteousness in an age in which faith in both was growing weak, and Jingoism, with its lust of war and rapine, was taking possession of the world. . . . Very striking is the contrast between Gladstone's career and that of his principal rival, who gave his mind little to practical improvement, and almost entirely to the game of party and the struggle for power. Gladstone was, in the best sense, a man of the people; and the heart of the people seldom failed to respond to his appeal.

Goldwin Smith, *My Memory of Gladstone*

From *Fun*,] [Oct. 25, 1882.
STATUE OF THE VOCAL MEMNON,
Carved in Gladstone; said to emit sweet melodies when gilded by the rays of the rising sun.

16 A cartoon of Gladstone, 1892

Comment

William Ewart Gladstone, the son of a wealthy Liverpool merchant, was educated at Eton and Oxford where, as President of the Union, he quickly established his reputation as a brilliant debater. Although he had held office under Peel (1841–46), he finally joined the Liberals after the Conservative party had broken up over the Corn Laws. (See Document 18.) His natural ability and keen mind soon brought him to the fore. He served as chancellor of the exchequer almost continuously from 1852 to 1866 under Aberdeen, Palmerston and Russell, and was prime minister on four occasions: 1868–74, 1880–85, 1886, 1892–94. A great believer in liberty, he acted with courage and a strong sense of Christian conviction.

Questions

a. In what ways does the writer of this extract illustrate Gladstone's physical strength and stamina?

b. How did Gladstone manage to keep himself physically fit for all his political work?

c. What proof is there here that Gladstone had an extremely able mind?

d. What other personal qualities of Gladstone are brought out in this account?

e. How does Smith compare the motives of Gladstone with those of Disraeli?

26 The Education Act, 1870

Be it enacted . . .

5. There shall be provided for every school district a sufficient amount of accommodation in public elementary schools available for all the children resident in such district for whose elementary education efficient and suitable provision is not otherwise made . . .

6. Where the Education Department are satisfied and have given public notice that there is an insufficient amount of public school accommodation for any school district, a school board shall be formed for such district and shall supply such difficiency . . .

7. . . . every public elementary school shall be conducted in accordance with the following regulations, namely,

    (i) no child shall be required, as a condition of being admitted into or continuing in the school, to attend or to abstain from attending any Sunday school, or any place of religious worship . . .

    (ii) the time or times during which any religious observance is practised or instruction in religious subjects is given at any meeting of the school shall be either at the beginning or at the end of such meeting . . . and any scholar may be withdrawn by his parent . . .

    (iii) the school shall be open at all times to the inspection of any of Her Majesty's inspectors . . .

17. Every child attending a school provided by any school board shall pay such weekly fee as may be prescribed by the school board, but the school board may remit the whole or any part of such fee in the case of any child when they are of the opinion that the parent of such child is unable from poverty to pay the same . . .

71. Every school board . . . may make byelaws . . .

    (i) requiring the parents of children of such age, not less than five years nor more than thirteen years, as may be fixed by the byelaws, to cause such children (unless there is some reasonable excuse) to attend school;

    (ii) determining the time during which children are so to attend school . . .

Comment

Before 1870 education opportunities for poorer children were largely limited to dame schools, sunday schools and church schools run by the National Society (Anglican) or the British and Foreign Society (non-conformist). The government had shown some interest by offering a grant to these society schools in 1833 and by setting up a Committee of the Privy Council in 1839 to supervise the use of the money provided. Large areas of the population, however, were still outside the scope of even the most elementary education. Church schools alone were clearly not sufficient to satisfy the need, made even more urgent by the passing of the 1867 Reform Bill (which had given the vote to town workers). The Education Act of 1870, drafted by W. E. Forster, laid the foundations of state education.

Questions

a. Under what circumstances was a School Board to be established?
b. Which children qualified for the Board Schools?
c. What control did the government have over these schools?
d. Why were religious services and instruction to take place at the beginning or end of a school session and not in the middle?
e. What do you understand by an *elementary* school?
f. Was education made (i) free, (ii) compulsory by this Act? Give reasons for your answer.
g. Why was it left to the School Boards to fix their own requirements on ages and hours?

27 The Criminal Law Amendment Act, 1871

Be it enacted . . .

Every person who shall do any one or more of the following acts, that is to say,

(1) use violence to any person or any property,

(2) threaten or intimidate any person in such manner as would justify a justice of the peace, on complaint made to him, to bind over the person so threatening or intimidating to keep the peace,

(3) molest or obstruct any person in manner defined by this section, with a view to coerce such person, —

    (i) being a master to dismiss or to cease to employ any workman, or being a workman to quit any employment or to return work before it is finished;

    (ii) being a master not to offer or being a workman not to accept any employment or work;

    (iii) being a master or workman to belong or not to belong to any trade union;

    (iv) being a master or workman to pay any fine or penalty imposed by any trade union;

    (v) being a master to alter the mode of carrying on his business, or the number or description of any persons employed by him,

shall be liable to imprisonment, with or without hard labour, for a term not exceeding three months.

A person shall, for the purposes of this Act, be deemed to molest or obstruct another person in any of the following cases; that is to say.

(1) if he persistently follow such person about from place to place;

(2) if he hide any tools, clothes, or other property owned or used by such person, or deprive him of, or hinder him in the use thereof;

(3) if he watch or beset the house or other place where such person resides or works or carries on business, or happens to be, or the approach to such house or place, or if with two or more other persons he follow such person in a disorderly manner in or through any street or road.

Comment

From 1850 there had been a rapid growth of New Model Unions, highly organised bodies which drew their members from the ranks of the skilled workers. A 'Junta' had been formed by the full-time secretaries of five of these unions to apply joint pressure on political parties. When, therefore, after a court dispute in 1867, the judge declared that trade union funds were not covered by law, the Junta successfully lobbied Gladstone's government. The Trade Union Act of 1871, which gave full legal protection to their funds, represented a considerable victory. Their joy, however, was short-lived. The Criminal Law Amendment Act, passed shortly afterwards, again undermined their powers and ensured that in future they would look to the Conservative party for support.

Questions

a. What main methods of persuasion used by trade unions were made illegal by the passing of this Act?

b. In what ways were masters protected by this Act?

c. In what ways were individual workmen protected by this Act?

d. Could the gates of a factory during a strike be picketed *peacefully* after the passing of this Act?

e. What was the main effect of this Act on the power of trade unions?

f. Do you feel that a trade union has the right to force
   (i) its members to take part in a strike?
   (ii) its employers to dismiss a workman who is not a trade union member?

17 A meeting of the Trade
Unions

18 A Trade Union
membership card

Trade Unions

Comment

The growth of large unions in the nineteenth century inevitably aroused the fear and opposition of employers. Although the New Model Unions did much to reassure public opinion by their well-organised and peaceful approach, various attempts were made to restrict their powers. (See Documents 27, 34 and 45.)

Questions

a. Examine Plate 17.
  (i) What did the cartoonist see as the aims of the trade unions?
  (ii) What sort of people did he portray as typical members?
b. Examine Plate 18.
  (i) What sort of people were portrayed as typical members by the drawings on this trade union membership card?
  (ii) What did *it* see as the aims of the Trade Union?

28 The Licensing Act, 1872

Whereas it is expedient to amend the law . . . for the sale of intoxicating liquors and the better prevention of drunkenness: Be it enacted . . .

3. No person shall sell or expose for sale by retail any intoxicating liquor without being duly licensed to sell the same . . .

12. Every person who in any highway or other public place, whether a building or not, is guilty while drunk of riotous or disorderly behaviour, or who is drunk while in charge on any highway of any carriage, horse, cattle, or steam engine, or who is drunk when in possession of any loaded fire-arms, may be apprehended and shall be liable to a penalty not exceeding forty shillings, or . . . to imprisonment with or without hard labour for any term not exceeding one month . . .

13. If any licensed person knowingly permits drunkenness or any violent, quarrelsome, or riotous conduct to take place on his premises, or knowingly sells any intoxicating liquor to a drunken person, he shall be liable to a penalty not exceeding for the first offence ten pounds.

20. . . . Every person who knowingly sells or keeps or exposes for sale any intoxicating liquor mixed with any harmful ingredient shall be liable for the first offence to a penalty not exceeding twenty pounds . . . (and) shall, unless his license is forfeited for such offence, affix on such part of his premises . . . a plaquard stating his conviction . . .

25. . . . all premises on which intoxicating liquors are sold shall be closed as follows; that is to say,

If such premises are situated within the city of London . . . on Sunday, Christmas Day, and Good Friday during the whole day up to one of the clock in the afternoon, and between the hours of three and six of the clock in the afternoon, and between the hours of eleven of the clock at night and five of the clock on the following morning; and on all other days between twelve of the clock at night and five of the clock on the following morning . . .

Comment

Drunkenness presented a real problem in most industrial towns and offended the Christian conscience of Victorian England. Churches made a considerable effort to combat this evil by forming Temperance Societies to discourage their members from acquiring the habit. The Liberal party, which contained a large number of non-conformists, supported the Licensing Act to control the sale of alcohol. Outside the party it was very unpopular — especially with the brewers, who were both powerful and influential. Gladstone in fact claimed later that, in his defeat at the 1874 election, he had been brought down 'in a torrent of gin and beer'.

Questions

a. What do you think Gladstone's motives were in passing this Act? (See also Document 25.)

b. Under what circumstances could a person be arrested for drunkenness?

c. In what way did the Act help to make the licensee responsible for the control of drunkenness?

d. What sort of ingredients, do you think, had previously been mixed with liquor? How did the Act seek to discourage licensees from continuing this practice?

e. What restrictions were placed on the sale of intoxicating liquors? How do these compare with present-day restrictions?

f. What are the arguments for and against restricted licensing hours? What is the practice in other countries?

29 General Gordon and the Sudan, 1884

September 19th. Stewart will bear witness that my whole efforts have been, and will be, directed to carry out my instructions, viz., the withdrawal of the garrisons and refugees. . . . I did not escape with Stewart simply because the people would not have been such fools as to have let me go. . . . Even if they had been willing for me to go, I would not have gone and left them in their misery. . . . I am deeply grateful to those who have prayed for us. Any expeditionary force that may come up comes up for the honour of England, and England will be grateful . . .

I own to having been very insubordinate to Her Majesty's Government and its officials, but it is my nature and I cannot help it. I know if *I* was chief I would never employ *myself*, for I am incorrigible. To men like Dilke, who weigh every word, I must be *perfect poison*. I wonder what the telegrams about Soudan have cost Her Majesty's Government?

December 12th–13th. Small church parade. I sincerely hope this will be the last we shall have to witness. . . . The Arabs fired two shells at the Palace; one burst in the air, the other fell in the water in a direct line with the window I was sitting at, distant about a hundred yards.

December 13th. The steamers went up and attacked the Arabs at Bourré (certainly this day-after-day delay has a most disheartening effect on every one. Today is the 276th day of our anxiety). The Arabs appear, by all accounts, to have suffered today heavily at Bourré. We had none wounded by the Arabs; but one man, by the discharge of a bad cartridge, got a cut in the neck; this was owing to the same cause as nearly blew out my eyes the other day. We are going to send down the *Bordeen* the day after tomorrow, and with her I shall send this Journal. If some effort is not made before ten days' time the town will fall. It is inexplicable, this delay. If the Expeditionary Forces have reached the river and met my steamers, one hundred men are all that we require, just to show themselves. . . . I have done my best for the honour of our country. Good bye.

The Journals of Major-Gen. C. G. Gordon at Khartoum

Comment

In 1882 Gladstone had reluctantly sent an expedition to Egypt to suppress a military revolt and thus protect British interests in the area (i.e. the Suez Canal, etc.). After the war the British army remained and Sir Evelyn Baring was sent as adviser to the khedive (the ruler of Egypt). When therefore the Sudan (a territory owned by Egypt) rose up against the injustices of its overlords, the British insisted that Egyptian garrisons should be withdrawn. Gladstone had no wish to involve his army in the wastes and deserts of the Sudan. He did, however, send General Gordon, who had personal knowledge of the natives, to undertake the difficult task of effecting the withdrawal. Gordon, an impulsive man, disobeyed the instructions and decided to defend Khartoum, which was quickly surrounded. After much delay, Gladstone sent a relief expedition which arrived on 27 January 1885 — two days after the fall of the city and the death of Gordon. Public opinion was enraged and bitter attacks made on the government.

Questions

a. Why had Gordon been sent into the Sudan?
b. What reasons does he give for not escaping from Khartoum?
c. How friendly were his relations with the British government?
d. Is there any evidence to show that Gordon was a religious man?
e. What other of his personal qualities are illustrated by this extract?
f. Is there anything here to suggest that the Arabs were not very good fighters?
g. What factors tended (i) to lower morale, (ii) to raise morale in Khartoum during the final stages of the siege?

30 Ireland, 1886

A twenty-one years' lease granted to the present tenant's father in 1860 fixed the rent at about £410. The son succeeded while this lease was running, and in 1876 or 1877 became anxious for a new lease. . . . The new lease was not granted, and accordingly the tenant sought to register under the Land Act of 1870 his permanent improvements. These improvements were mainly under the following heads: Blasting, sledging and removing stones; levelling old ditches and making new ones; building sewers; making main and minor drains; sinking wells and repairing roads. There were also building improvements . . . there was an enclosure wall, a new granary, steamhouse and cowsheds, workmen's lodge and piggeries. The tenants' accounts showed an expenditure on these and other items of over £2000.

But the landlord contested the right to register these improvements. A lawsuit arose, which ended with the decision that the improvements could be registered, but not the amount of money spent on them. The lawsuit cost the tenant £500. This lease expired a few months before the Land Act of 1881 was passed. No renewal had taken place, and the tenant was served with a notice of eviction, under the pressure of which he accepted a sixty years' lease, at a rent of £380.

H. S. Wilkinson, *The Eve of Home Rule — Impression of Ireland in 1886*

It is only a sense of the gravity of this issue which induces me, at a period of life when nature cries aloud for repose to seek, after sitting in thirteen parliaments, a seat in a fourteenth . . .

Two clear, positive, intelligible plans are before the world. There is the plan of the Government; and there is the plan of Lord Salisbury. Our plan is that Ireland should, under well-considered conditions, transact her own affairs. His plan is to ask Parliament for new repressive laws, and to enforce them resolutely for twenty years; at the end of which time he assures us that Ireland will be fit to accept any gifts, in the way of local government or the repeal of the co-ercion laws, that you may wish to give her . . .

Gladstone's Address to the Electors of Midlothian, June 1886

Comment

By 1886 the Irish problem had reached its climax. Catholic Emancipation (see Document 4) and grants for education (see Document 17) had failed to soothe the growing volume of discontent. So, too, had Gladstone's efforts to remove the grievances of tenant farmers. His first Land Act (1870) had ordered compensation to be given for improvements to farms, while his second Land Act (1881) had not only set up a court to fix fair rents, but had also offered loans to help with the purchase of holdings. Nevertheless, the Irish themselves were determined to settle for nothing short of Home Rule. Gladstone was finally converted and introduced the first Home Rule Bill in 1886. This met with bitter opposition and was eventually rejected in the Commons by 30 votes.

Questions

a. What type of farming was practised on the farm in the first extract? How up to date were their methods of farming?

b. Why do you think the son wanted to renew his lease some years before the old one expired?

c. Why did the landlord refuse to renew the lease at this stage? How did he eventually turn the situation to his own advantage?

d. Why did the tenant wish to register his permanent improvements under the Land Act of 1870?

e. Why did so few tenants challenge unscrupulous landlords in the law courts?

f. How would the Land Act of 1881 have helped the tenant in this case?

g. What 'well-considered conditions' did Gladstone have in mind in his plan for Irish Home Rule?

h. What alternative proposals did the Conservatives have for the solution of the Irish problem?

IRISH PANTOMIME.
The sausage-machine trick; or, converting Land Leaguers into good wholesome subjects.

19 Irish Pantomime

20 'Soothing the savage breast'

21 The Old Pump

Three cartoons of Gladstone, published in 1892

"SOOTHING THE SAVAGE BREAST."

THE OLD PUMP.
" Nothing to be got out of it, William."

Gladstone and Ireland

Comment

These cartoons illustrate Gladstone's various attempts to solve the Irish problem. (See also Documents 30 and 44.)

Questions

How do these cartoons explain the details of Gladstone's Irish policy:
a. in 1880? (See Plate 19.)
b. in 1881? (See Plate 20.)
c. after 1885? (See Plate 21.)

31 Disraeli

Never in public life in either hemisphere were there confronted two men more diametrically opposed in manner and mode of thought than Disraeli and Gladstone. They had only one thing in common — genius. . . . Hitherto, through a turbulent life, he (Disraeli) had a dual battle to fight. There were his political adversaries in the Liberal camp: his worst, most dangerous, foes were those of his own household. For more than thirty years he had been suspect, an undesirable alien among the Tory party, to which he, after due consideration finally decided to attach himself. His supreme gifts made him indispensable to them. None the less they distrusted and disliked him. Even after he came into his own, Prime Minister and Leader of a party he, as he boasted, had educated, there was evidence in the House of Commons of the old, deeply rooted feeling.

. . . Lord Rowton, long time his private secretary, told me his chief utilised what otherwise might have been wasted moments in the Division Lobby by soldering any little cracks apparent in the Ministerial forces. If the Whips notified to him sign of revolt in a particular quarter, the Premier, watching the throng pass through the Division Lobby, would nod recognition to the discontented member, engage him in conversation whilst the Lobby emptied, and, if the case were at all threatening, link arms and lead him on to the wicket where the tellers stand. 'I never', said Lord Rowton, 'knew of a brooding mutiny come to a head after the Chief had walked out of the Lobby arm-in-arm with the leading spirit' . . .

Disraeli lacked two qualities, failing which true eloquence is impossible. He was never quite in earnest, and he was not troubled by dominating conviction. . . . He was endowed with a lively fancy and cultivated the art of coining phrases, generally personal in their bearing. When these were flashed forth he delighted the House. For the rest, at the period I knew him, when he had grown respectable and was weighted with responsibility, he was often dull. There were, indeed, few things more dreary than a long speech from Dizzy. At short, sharp replies to questions designed to be embarrassing he was effective.

H. W. Lucy, *Sixty Years in the Wilderness*

22

'Pulled up at last. P.C. Dizzy—"It's no use sir. I've strict orders from the country not to let anything of this sort pass". The Leader of the Opposition checked in a would-be wild career'

Comment

Benjamin Disraeli had none of the traditional marks of the English statesman. He came from a Jewish family of Italian extraction and had not even been sent to public school and university. Nevertheless, he became an M.P. in 1837 and was prominent enough to lead the rebellious group of Conservatives who opposed Peel on the Corn Laws. He then served under Lord Derby as chancellor of the exchequer before becoming prime minister for a brief spell in 1868. His main ministry lasted from 1874 to 1880, during which time he was created Earl of Beaconsfield.

Questions

a. Why was Disraeli disliked so much by members of his own party?
b. How, under these circumstances, had he therefore managed to become leader of the Conservative party?
c. What methods did he use to keep his party united?
d. Why do you think Disraeli made so many personal enemies among the Liberal party?
e. Why were his speeches never completely convincing?
f. What do you think had made Disraeli 'respectable' after 1873 (when Lucy knew him)?
g. Examine Plate 22, a cartoon dated 1874. Who is the policeman? Why is he refusing to allow the carriage to pass?

32 Tory Democracy

Gentlemen, some years ago the Tory party experienced a great over-throw. I am here to admit that in my opinion it was deserved. A long course of power and prosperity had induced it to sink into a state of apathy and indifference. . . . Instead of the principles professed by Mr. Pitt and Lord Grenville, the Tory system had degenerated into a policy which found an adequate basis on the principles of exclusiveness and restriction. Gentlemen, the Tory party, unless it is a national party is nothing. It is not a confederacy of nobles, it is not a democratic multitude; it is a party formed from all the numerous classes in the realm . . .

Now, I have always been of opinion that the Tory party has three great objects. The first is to maintain the institutions of the country. . . . The discontent upon the subject of the representation . . . was termin-ated by the Act of Parliamentary Reform of 1867–8. That Act was founded on a confidence that the great body of the people of this country were 'Conservative'. When I say 'Conservative', I use the word in its purest and loftiest sense. I mean that the people of England, and especially the working classes of England, are proud of belonging to a great country . . . that they believe, on the whole, that the greatness and the empire of England are to be attributed to the ancient institutions of the land . . .

Gentlemen, there is another and second great object of the Tory party — to uphold the Empire of England. . . . Another great object of the Tory party is the elevation of the condition of the people. . . . I ventured to say that the health of the people was the most important question for a statesman. . . . It involves the state of the dwellings of the poor. It involves their enjoyment of some of the chief elements of nature — air, light and water. It involves the regulation of their industry, the inspection of their toil. It involves the purity of their provisions. . . . Well, it may be the 'policy of sewage' to a Liberal member of Parliament. But to one of the labouring population of England . . . it is not a 'policy of sewage', but a question of life and death . . .

Disraeli's speech at Crystal Palace, June 1872

23 A cartoon on
Reform, published
in *Punch*, 1867

A LEAP IN THE DARK.

Comment

Disraeli first made his name as a novelist, writing *Vivian Grey* as early as
1827. It was, however, in his book *Coningsby* (1844) that he first outlined his idea of a Tory democracy. The Conservatives, he felt, were the
natural leaders of the working classes (as opposed to the middle-class
Liberals) and should take the lead in reform. When eventually he held
high office, he put some of these theories into practice by introducing the
Reform Bill (1867), as well as a series of measures on public health,
housing, education and trade unions. His aim was to bridge the gap
between 'the two nations' — the rich and the poor.

Questions

a. Over what issue had the Tory party experienced 'a great overthrow'
earlier in the century?
b. How long, in fact, had the Tories been in power before their defeat?
Who had been their leaders during that period?
c. Why, according to Disraeli, had the old Tory party deservedly fallen
from power?
d. What did he mean by saying that the party should be 'a national
party'?
e. What did he mean by the word 'conservative'?

33 The Artisans' Dwellings Act, 1875

Whereas various portions of many cities and boroughs are so built, and the buildings thereon are so densely inhabited, as to be highly injurious to the moral and physical welfare of the inhabitants: And whereas there are in such portions of cities and boroughs as aforesaid a great number of houses, courts, and alleys which, by reason of the want of light, air, ventilation, or of proper conveniences, or from other causes, are unfit for human habitation, and fevers and diseases are constantly generated there, causing death and loss of health, not only in the courts and alleys but also in other parts of such cities and boroughs;

And whereas it often happens that owing to the above circumstances, and to the fact that such houses, courts, and alleys are the property of several owners, it is not in the power of any one owner to make such alterations as are necessary for the public health:

And whereas it is necessary for the public health that many such houses, courts, and alleys should be pulled down, and such portions of the said cities and boroughs should be reconstructed; . . . Be it enacted. . . . Where an official representation is made to the local Authority that any houses, courts or alleys within a certain area . . . are unfit for human habitation, or that diseases indicating a generally low condition of health amongst the population have been from time to time prevalent in a certain area . . . the local Authority shall take such representation into their consideration, and if satisfied of the truth thereof, and of the sufficiency of their resources, shall pass a resolution to the effect that such area is an unhealthy area, and that an improvement scheme ought to be made in respect of such area, and after passing such a resolution shall forthwith proceed to make a scheme for the improvement of such area.

24 'Over London
by rail' by Doré,
1873

Comment

The Industrial Revolution had quickly thrown up the most dreadful
slums in many of the major cities. Back-to-back houses had been built
around small courtyards by speculative builders with little thought for
either ventilation or sanitary arrangements. Frequently overcrowded,
they became the breeding-ground for disease. Town planning was un-
heard of at this time and local authorities, often dominated by property-
owners, took little interest. In 1868, however, the Artisans' Dwellings
Act gave councils the right to condemn and demolish individual houses
which were known to be unhealthy. This only touched lightly on the
problem. Whole slum areas needed to be cleared if real progress was
to be made. The Act of 1875 was introduced by Disraeli's home
secretary, Cross.

Questions

a. What facilities were lacking in so many houses which made them
'unfit for human habitation'?
b. Why did fevers and diseases spread so rapidly in these places?
c. Why was it impossible for an individual owner of a house in such an
area to make improvements?
d. What other power was given to local authorities by this Act?
e. Examine Plate 24, a drawing of London in 1873. What do we learn
from this picture about the health and housing standards of
working-class homes?

34 Conspiracy and Protection of Property Act, 1875

Be it enacted . . .

3. An agreement or combination by two or more persons to do or procure to be done any act in contemplation or furtherance of a trade dispute between employers and workmen shall not be indictable as a conspiracy if such act committed by one person would not be punishable as a crime . . .

   Nothing in this section shall affect the law relating to riot, unlawful assembly, breach of the peace, or sedition, or any offence against the State or the Sovereign . . .

5. Where any person wilfully and maliciously breaks a contract of service, knowing or having reasonable cause to believe that the probable consequences of his doing, either alone on in combination with others, will be to endanger human life, or cause serious bodily injury, or to expose valuable property whether real or personal to destruction or serious injury, he shall on conviction thereof . . . be liable either to pay a penalty not exceeding twenty pounds, or to be imprisoned for a term not exceeding three months, with or without hard labour . . .

8. Every person who, with a view to compel any other person to abstain from doing or to do any act which such other person has a legal right to do or abstain from doing, shall use violence to any person or any property, or shall threaten or intimidate any person . . . and every person who, with a view seriously to annoy or intimidate any other person, shall persistently follow such other person about or hide any property owned or used by such other person . . . shall be liable to a fine not exceeding twenty pounds, or to imprisonment not exceeding three months . . .

14. The Criminal Law Amendment Act, 1871, shall be and is hereby repealed . . .

Comment

The 'Junta' of trade union leaders had organised opposition to Liberal candidates at the election of 1874, following Gladstone's unfriendly ruling over the question of strike pickets. (See Document 27.) Disraeli rewarded his newly-found supporters by repealing the Criminal Law Amendment Act and passing instead the Conspiracy and Protection of Property Act. This gave a favourable interpretation to their legal position both on conspiracy and on picketing. Strikes could now be made effective without fear of prosecution.

Questions

a. Explain what you understand by the terms (i) conspiracy, (ii) indictable, (iii) real and personal property.
b. In what way did this Act give protection to trade unions from the law of conspiracy?
c. Under what circumstances were strikes made illegal?
d. What groups of workers were therefore not allowed to strike under the terms of this Act? Give examples.
e. What methods of persuading fellow workers to join a strike were still regarded as illegal by this Act?
f. What type of persuasion was now made legal? Compare Section 8 of this Act with the Criminal Law Amendment Act. (See Document 27.)

35 The Bulgarian Atrocities

It may seem that one, who is no more than a private individual, is guilty of presumption in dealing with so great and perilous a question. But I have a great faith in the power of opinion, of the opinion of civilised and Christian Europe. It can remove mountains. Six months ago, England and Europe had just learned, upon official authority, the reality and extent of the Massacres, and of outrages far worse than Massacre in Bulgaria. . . . The belief that a Government in alliance with Her Majesty could stand in close complicity with crimes so foul was a belief so startling, nay, so horrible, that it was not fit to be entertained, unless upon the clearest and fullest evidence. . . . We now have to confront a fact, more revolting than the fact of the Massacres themselves. The acts of the Porte, through nine long months, demonstrate a deliberate intention. That purpose has been to cover up iniquity; to baffle enquiry; to reward prominence in crime; to prolong the reign of terror . . .

Mr. Baring reports on Sept. 26, four months after the Massacres, 'no visible improvement has taken place in the condition of the Bulgarian villagers. . . . The inhabitants of the burnt villages stand so much in dread of the Pomaks that they dare not go to the forests to cut wood for new dwellings; whilst the Pomaks make continual raids on the shelterless people, and take what few things they possess. Mr. Brophy reports from Bourgas how on July 21 eight Circassians attacked a Bulgarian family at midnight. The father and son were pricked with daggers to obtain money: the daughter, of thirteen or fourteen, was twice violated. 'On every side the Bulgarians are robbed, beaten, or killed, by their Circassian or Turkish neighbours. The rayahs are in many places afraid to go to their fields to plough, or to the mill to get their corn ground. The Mussulmans of all races seem to consider that it is lawful to despoil the "infidel" in every way, and if the "infidel" dare to resist, to murder him' . . .

The British Ambassador has been possessed with the belief that the condition of the subject races of Turkey ought to be supremely determined by whatever our estimate of British interests may require. A little faith in the ineradicable difference between right and wrong is worth a great deal of European diplomacy . . .

Rt. Hon. W. E. Gladstone, *Lessons in Massacre*

Comment

Disraeli feared that the decline of the Turkish Empire would give Russia the vital opportunity to expand into the Mediterranean, an area vital to British trade. He therefore gave support to the sultan in the hope of keeping the Turkish Empire intact as a barrier against Russian ambition. This, however, raised problems. In 1875 Bosnia and Herzegovina rose up in rebellion against the sultan's corrupt government. Although Russia, Germany and Austria together urged the Turks to reform, Disraeli refused to join them for fear of weakening Turkey. Then, in 1876, the world was horrified by the brutal massacres which took place after further rebellions in Bulgaria, Serbia and Montenegro. Many of the victims were Christians. Gladstone thundered out against both the Turks and the British government in a series of speeches and pamphlets, demanding that the Turks should be expelled 'bag and baggage' from Bulgaria.

Questions

a. Why had Gladstone originally felt that the Turkish government could not possibly have been involved in the massacres?
b. What four accusations does Gladstone make here against that government?
c. What types of violence did the Bulgarian Christians continue to suffer even after the massacres?
d. How was their everyday life being affected by this reign of terror?
e. What was the attitude of the British government, as reflected by its ambassador?
f. Why was Gladstone so confident that these atrocities would finally be stopped?
g. Do you agree with Disraeli that 'British interests' are the most important consideration in matters of foreign policy — or with Gladstone that the choice between 'right and wrong' is the most vital factor?

36 The Congress of Berlin, 1878

For the moment he seemed to have achieved a diplomatic success, and he told the crowd which greeted him on his arrival in London, 'I have brought you back peace, but peace, I hope, with honour, and such a peace as will satisfy our sovereign and gratify the country'. I saw and watched the crowd, and can testify that its enthusiasm was by no means excessive. Still for the moment the Berlin treaty had increased the popularity of the Government.

In the House of Lords the Prime Minister delivered a speech in vindication of the settlement made at the Berlin congress. This may be described as the crowning moment of his career. Rarely has the head of the Government addressed such an audience. Four princes of the blood were present. . . . Nearly all the eminent politicians in both Houses gathered to hear Lord Beaconsfield. He spoke for an hour and thirty-five minutes, and it was his greatest oratorical success — indeed, I think his one oratorical success in the Upper House. It was a general vindication of the policy of the Government and especially of the treaty — 'the insane convention', Mr. Gladstone called it — under which we had agreed to guarantee the dominions of Turkey in Asia Minor against attack and had acquired the island of Cyprus as a place of arms. Experience has proved that the provisions of the Berlin treaty with regard to Turkey rested on a very shaky foundation. Most of them have since been set aside or superceded, and the agreement for the defence of Asia Minor has never been more than a piece of waste paper. The one solid result of the manoeuvres of diplomacy for these months of June and July was the acquisition of Cyprus, and that has proved for the object for which it was acquired to be absolutely worthless.

W. Jeans, *Parliamentary Reminiscences*

Comment

Disraeli's failure to bring pressure to bear on the Turks in Bulgaria (see Document 35), finally provoked Russia into acting single-handed. War was declared in 1877. Although Disraeli threatened action against Russia by moving a fleet into the area, he could not prevent them

25 'A blaze of triumph!',
published in Punch, 1878

from signing the Treaty of San Stephano with Turkey in 1878. This established a large independent state of Bulgaria, which stretched down to the sea and was clearly destined to become a Russian puppet state. Disraeli finally managed to persuade all the powers (Britain, Germany, Austria, France and Russia) to discuss the whole question at the Berlin Congress. This in itself was a fine diplomatic achievement.

Questions

a. What do you think were the political views of the writer of this extract? Give your reasons.

b. Why did the Congress of Berlin increase the popularity of Disraeli's government?

c. Why was Disraeli so interested in protecting the Turkish Empire?

d. Do you agree that this policy 'rested on a very shaky foundation'? Why?

e. What were Gladstone's views on the Treaty? Why was he so opposed to giving support to Turkey? (See also Document 36.)

f. How does this extract illustrate Disraeli's qualities as a statesman and politician?

g. Examine Plate 25, which is a *Punch* cartoon dated 1878. Who is the man on the tight-rope? What does the man on his back represent? Explain the references to 'war' and 'peace' on the pole.

37 Moonlighting in Ireland, 1887

The Daily News, 16 February 1887

Three months since, or thereabouts, two brothers named Lynch were evicted at Clenagh Castle, about four miles from Ballycar, for non-payment of rent. They were tenants on the estate of Mrs. O'Grady, and since the period of their eviction emergency bailiffs were in charge of the evicted farm. The bailiffs were in the habit of getting their supplies from Limerick, and last evening, expecting some by train from Limerick, they proceeded to the railway station, Acting-Sergeant O'Connor and Constable Dowling accompanying as an escort. On their return, and when a short distance from the railway station, a volley was fired at the policemen and the bailiff (John Byers) from either side of the road, the result being that the acting-sergeant and the bailiff were wounded, it is believed mortally, and Constable Dowling was also wounded, but not fatally. An alarm was raised, but the murderers made good their escape. No arrests have yet been made, but the police are searching the districts.

The Times, 18 February 1887

Driving into Ennis on Tuesday afternoon I met the unfortunate man John Byers, who had been mortally wounded the night before, being carried along in a wretched covered cart to the County Infirmary. He was quite unattended, except by an old hospital nurse and two armed policemen, who walked beside the cart to protect him from further mischief from the people, though he was then in a dying condition, no woman in the village of Newmarket daring to accompany him, or render him any assistance in his last moments. . . . In answer to my telegram of inquiry on Wednesday morning, one of the doctors writes: 'The poor man Byers died this morning at six o'clock. . . . I found it impossible to get a coffin at Ennis (so great is the influence of the League), and I had to procure one from the Property Defence Association. I can add nothing to this except that his wife was hissed on her arrival, and no accommodation could be found for her in the town. This shows the dreadful state of affairs brought about by the Land League in our country.

Comment

The Land League had been founded to counter the unfair demands of unscrupulous landlords in Ireland. 'No-rent' campaigns were organised, evictions were challenged in court and a plan of 'boycott' was practised on any who took over holdings from which members had been evicted. Parnell, who was both president of the League and leader of the Irish Nationalist Party in parliament, was against violence. But the movement soon got out of hand. 'Moonlighting' — murders and outrages committed at dead of night — became a weapon of terror.

Questions

a. Why had the Lynch brothers been evicted?
b. Why do you think the bailiffs obtained their supplies from Limerick and not locally?
c. What suggests that the bailiffs lived in a state of fear?
d. How does the second extract illustrate
  (i) the influence of the Land League on ordinary people;
  (ii) the *general* feeling of hostility towards landlords in the area?
e. In what ways did property-owners seek to protect themselves from the activities of the Land League?
f. What was the attitude of the police? What chance did they have of arresting the murderers?

38 The Birth of the Labour Party, 1900

The new movement did not begin auspiciously. At the end of the first year only 40 Trade Unions out of about 1200 then existing had affiliated, with a membership of 353,000. The great organisations of the miners and the textile workers stood aloof, looking on the new movement with suspicion and regarding it with undisguised hostility. The first Annual Conference was held in Manchester in February 1901, and I well remember the feeling of despondency which prevailed . . .

During the previous year (1900) a General Election had taken place. It came before the new Committee had had time to get into its work. The I.L.P. had nine candidates in the field, and the Trade Unions four. Of these only two were successful — Keir Hardie at Merthyr and Mr. Richard Bell at Derby . . .

Keir Hardie was again the solitary independent Labour member of the new Parliament. He used to describe himself as the United Labour Party. His return raised a financial problem for the National Council of the I.L.P. There was no payment of members from the National Exchequer in those days. Hardie had no Trade Union behind him, and the newly formed Labour Representative Committee had no funds. The National Council of the I.L.P. set to work to raise by a private appeal a sum of £150 a year towards his support . . .

Hardie had no private means. He was running *The Labour Leader*, but that was a burden rather than a source of income. I have a letter from him written to me at this time in which he puts his financial position frankly before me. He paid fourteen shillings a week for rooms in London, his food and other expenses he put at a pound a week, secretarial help and postage cost him fifteen shillings. In addition he had to provide for his home in Scotland, and for clothing and railway fares. To meet these necessary expenses, which his £150 allowance was far short of meeting, he was obliged to take meetings at week-ends and almost nightly during the Parliamentary recess. These were the circumstances of the first Independent Labour M.P.

Philip Viscount Snowden, *An Autobiography*, Vol. I, pp. 93–5

26
Keir Hardie speaks
in favour of the
suffragettes at a
meeting in
Trafalgar Square
in 1913

Comment

The Reform Acts of 1867 and 1884 had created a large working-class electorate, which the Board schools set up in 1870 were attempting to educate. (See Document 26.) The need for a new political party to represent their interests in parliament gradually became apparent. Although an Independent Labour party had been formed by a group of socialists in 1893, its initial impact was slight. By 1899, however, trade unionists were becoming seriously alarmed at the growing attacks made on their position by employers. It was therefore decided, following a meeting of the T.U.C. in 1899, to establish a Labour Representation Committee (the L.R.C.) to provide working-class candidates for parliament.

Questions

a. What percentage of the trade unions had affiliated to the L.R.C. by 1901?

b. Why do you think the miners and textile workers refused to join?

c. Why did the L.R.C. do so badly in the election of 1900?

d. Why did Hardie's election raise 'a financial problem'?

e. How, in fact, was Hardie supported in parliament?

f. How much was his *monthly* allowance? How much were his *monthly* expenses in London? What additional expenses did he have?

g. Examine Plate 26. How effective do you think Keir Hardie was as a speaker? What types of people are in his audience?

h. Why was the L.R.C. at such a disadvantage when compared with the Conservative and Liberal parties? How far had their position been improved by 1914? (See also Document 45.)

39 The Relief of Ladysmith

Buller now began his fourth attempt to relieve Ladysmith. The garrison was in dire straits, and for all of us, relievers and besieged, it was kill or cure. . . . In the course of the next two days he got his army thoroughly clumped-up in the maze of hills and spurs beyond Colenso. In these unfavourable conditions, without any turning movement, he assaulted the long-prepared, deeply-entrenched Boer position before Pieters. . . . It was four o'clock when the Irish Brigade began to toil up the steep sides of what is now called Inniskilling Hill, and sunset approached before the assault was delivered by the Inniskilling and Dublin Fusiliers. The spectacle was tragic. Through our glasses we could see the Boers' heads and slouch hats in miniature silhouette, wreathed and obscured by shell-bursts, against the evening sky. Up the bare grassy slopes slowly climbed the brown figures and glinting bayonets of the Irishmen, and the rattle of intense musketry drummed in our ears. The climbing figures dwindled; they ceased to move; they vanished into the darkening hillside. Out of twelve hundred men who assaulted, both Colonels, three majors, twenty officers and six hundred soldiers had fallen killed or wounded. The repulse was complete. . . . Hundreds of wounded lying on Inniskilling Hill suffered a cruel ordeal. The plight of these poor men between the firing lines without aid or water, waving pitiful strips of linen in mute appeal, was hard to witness. The Boers refused a formal truce, but invited doctors and stretcher-bearers to come without fear and collect the wounded and bury the dead.

February 27 was the anniversary of Majuba, and on this day the Natal army delivered its final attack. . . . First Barton's Hill was stormed; and lastly the dreaded position of the Inniskilling Hill was carried by the bayonet. . . . The Boers were in full retreat. . . . I rode with these two Squadrons, and galloped across the scrub-dotted plain, fired at only by a couple of Boer guns. Suddenly from the brushwood up rose gaunt figures waving hands of welcome. On we pressed, and at the head of a battered street of tin-roofed houses met Sir George White on horseback, faultlessly attired. Then we all rode together into the long beleaguered, almost starved-out Ladysmith. It was a thrilling moment.

W. S. Churchill, *My Early Life*

27 The Boer War. Canadians storming a kopje

Comment

The Boer War, which broke out in 1899, did not turn out to be quite such a formality as the British had expected. Kruger's 80,000 troops, with German guns and an intimate knowledge of the difficult terrain, proved to be resolute fighters. They immediately took the initiative. British territory was invaded, Ladysmith and Kimberley were besieged and relief forces decisively beaten. Only when large reinforcements were sent out from Britain in 1900 under Roberts and Kitchener did fortunes begin to change. Ladysmith, Kimberley and Mafeking were all relieved and the Boer armies gradually driven back. Winston Churchill was a war correspondent at the time in South Africa.

Questions

a. What evidence is there here to suggest that Buller was guilty of bad generalship?

b. What percentage of the Irish attackers survived the assault on Inniskilling Hill?

c. How does this extract illustrate the methods of warfare and types of weapon employed in the Boer War?

d. Describe the geography of the area around Ladysmith.

e. What is there in the second paragraph to suggest that Ladysmith had endured a long siege?

f. What does this extract tell us about (i) the Boers, (ii) Sir George White?

g. Examine Plate 27. Describe the equipment and weapons used by these Canadian troops. Did the terrain hinder or help them in this assault?

28 Infantry crossing the Modder River with the aid of lifelines

29 A Boer picket on Spion Kop, January 1900

The Boer War

Comment

These illustrations are original photographs taken during the war.
(See also Document 39.)

Questions

a. Examine Plate 28. How are the British troops organising the crossing
   of the Modder River?
b. Examine Plate 29. Were the Boers better or worse equipped than the
   British soldiers?
c. Describe the character and appearance of the Boers in this picket.
d. What natural advantages did the Boers have over the British?

40 Chamberlain and Tariff Reform

Ladies and gentlemen, I am not afraid to come here to the home of Adam Smith and to combat free imports, and still less am I afraid to preach to you preference with our colonies. . . . I do not regard this as a party meeting. I am no longer a party leader. . . . What are our objects? They are two. In the first place, we all desire the maintenance and increase of the national strength and the prosperity of the United Kingdom. . . . Then, in the second place, our object is, or should be, the realisation of the greatest ideal which has ever inspired statesmen in any country or in any age — the creation of an Empire such as the world has never seen . . .

I want to prepare you now, while there is time, for a struggle . . . from which, if we emerge defeated, this country will lose its place, will no longer count among the great nations of the world — a struggle which we are asked to meet with antiquated weapons and with old-fashioned tactics. . . . If you will compare your trade in 1872, thirty years ago, with the trade of 1902 — the export trade — you will find that there has been a moderate increase of £22,000,000. That, I think, is something like $7\frac{1}{2}$ per cent. Meanwhile, the population has increased 30 per cent. . . . In the same time the increase in the United States of America was £110,000,000 and the increase in Germany was £56,000,000. In the United Kingdom our export trade has been practically stagnant for thirty years . . .

But now, there is one thing which follows — that is, that our Imperial trade is absolutely essential to our prosperity at the present time. If that trade declines, or if it does not increase in proportion to our population and to the loss of trade with foreign countries, then we sink at once into a fifth-rate nation . . .

Now I have told you what you are to gain by preference. You will gain the retention and the increase of your customers. You will gain work for the enormous number of those who are now unemployed; you will pave the way for a firmer and more enduring union of the Empire. What will it cost? What do the colonies ask? They ask a preference on their particular products . . . you must put a tax on food.

Joseph Chamberlain's speech in Glasgow, 6 October 1903

Comment

By 1860 Britain had become a free trade country — thanks largely to the work of Huskisson, Peel and Gladstone. Towards the end of the century, however, some people were beginning to doubt the wisdom of this policy in the face of growing competition from America, Germany and France. Britain was fast in danger of losing her lead in trade. Joseph Chamberlain, the colonial secretary (1895–1903), led the campaign for tariff reform. His plan was to impose duties on foreign goods but, at the same time, to build up trade with the Empire by granting its members preferential rates. After a split in the cabinet in 1903, he resigned from office but toured around the country on a great campaign for tariff reform.

Questions

a. Who was Adam Smith? What views had he put forward?
b. What positions had Chamberlain previously held in (i) the Liberal party, (ii) the Conservative party? Why was he 'no longer a party leader'?
c. What were Chamberlain's two main objects at the time of this speech in 1903?
d. What two reasons did Chamberlain give for suggesting that Britain's trade figures were serious in spite of 'a moderate increase'?
e. What, according to Chamberlain, would be the consequence of Britain's prolonged failure to increase her trade?
f. Explain exactly what system he had in mind when he talked about 'imperial preference'.
g. In what two ways would the ordinary worker be affected by his scheme?

41 The Entente Cordiale, 1903

We arrived at the station in the Bois de Boulogne, where we found President Loubet and a large number of officials. We drove in six carriages each drawn by four horses with postilions, and were escorted by a large number of French cavalry. There was an immense crowd in the streets and all along the Champs-Elysées. As regards myself in the last carriage I received anything but a pleasant ovation, for the cheers had become jeers by the time I came, and being in a red coat I was selected by the crowd for witticisms. There were cries of 'Vive Marchand!' and 'Vive Fashoda!', 'Vivent les Boers!' and occasionally 'Vive Jeanne d'Arc!', which seemed to be going back a long way in history . . .

It was at the Hôtel de Ville that the King made a short speech which entirely changed the whole atmosphere and brought all the French round at once . . . '. . . Je n'oublierai jamais ma visite à votre charmante ville, et je puis vous assurer que c'est avec le plus grand plaisir que je reviens à Paris, où je me trouve toujours comme si j'étais chez moi.'

The last phrase went home, and as he sat down he received a tremendous ovation. He seemed to have captured Paris by storm. From that moment everything was changed wherever we went. Not only the King but all of the suite were received with loud and repeated cheering. It was the most marvellous transformation, and all in three days. The first day distinctly antagonistic, the second cold, and finally frenzied enthusiasm . . .

The visit eventually had far-reaching effects, and it was all very well for Lord Lansdowne to claim afterwards the credit for the *Entente Cordiale*, but neither he nor the government could ever have got the French people round from hostility to enthusiastic friendship in the way King Edward did. As M. Paul Cambon, the French Ambassador in London, remarked, any clerk at the Foreign Office could draw up a treaty, but there was no one else who could have succeeded in producing the right atmosphere for a *rapprochement* with France.

Sir Frederick Ponsonby, *Recollections of Three Reigns*, pp. 169–73

30 Edward VII and the French president at the
Franco-British Exhibition, 1908

Comment

Bismarck had succeeded in setting up a powerful Triple Alliance
(Germany, Austria and Italy), which, in the hands of the Kaiser,
became an increasing threat to the peace of Europe. Under these
circumstances, France and Russia had signed a Dual Entente in 1894
to protect themselves from possible attack. Britain's earlier position of
'splendid isolation' was somewhat changed by Germany's mounting
rivalry in colonial and naval strength. Therefore, in spite of a history of
conflict, France and Britain eventually moved closer together. Edward
VII's visit to Paris in March 1903 was followed by the signing of the
Entente Cordiale (April 1904), through which outstanding differences
were finally settled. Ponsonby, who wrote this account, was assistant
private secretary to the king.

Questions

a. Explain the significance of the crowd's cries of 'Vive Fashoda' and
    'Vivent les Boers' as Ponsonby drove past.
b. Why were the French people so hostile to the British?
c. How did the King manage to change the feelings of the ordinary
    French people?
d. How does Ponsonby emphasise the suddenness of the change?
e. Who was Lord Lansdowne?
f. What were the terms of the Entente Cordiale? In what sense were
    the terms 'far-reaching'? (See also Plate 30.)

42 The Suffragettes, 1905

The life of the old Parliament, dominated for nearly twenty years by the Conservative Party, was drawing to an end, and the country was on the eve of a general election in which the Liberals hoped to be returned to power. Quite naturally the Liberal candidates went to the country with perfervid promises of reform in every possible direction. . . . We determined to address ourselves to those men who were likely to be in the Liberal Cabinet, demanding to know whether their reforms were going to include justice to women.

We laid our plans to begin this work at a great meeting to be held in Free Trade Hall, Manchester, with Sir Edward Grey as the principal speaker. . . . Annie Kenney and my daughter Christabel were charged with the mission of questioning Sir Edward Grey. They sat quietly through the meeting, at the close of which questions were invited. Several questions were asked by men and were courteously answered. Then Annie Kenney arose and asked: 'If the Liberal party is returned to power, will they take steps to give votes for women?' At the same time Christabel held aloft the little banner that everyone in the hall might understand the nature of the question. Sir Edward Grey returned no answer to Annie's question, and the men sitting near her forced her rudely into her seat, while a steward pressed his hat over her face . . .

Annie Kenney stood up in her chair and cried out over the noise of shuffling feet and murmurs of conversation: 'Will the Liberal Government give votes to women?' Then the audience became a mob. They howled, they shouted and roared, shaking their fists fiercely at the woman who dared to intrude her question into a man's meeting. . . . Flung into the streets, the two girls staggered to their feet and began to address the crowds. Within five minutes they were arrested on a charge of obstruction and, in Christabel's case, of assaulting the police. Both were summonsed to appear next morning in a police court, where, after a trial which was a mere farce, Annie Kenney was sentenced to pay a fine of five shillings, with an alternative of three days in prison, and Christabel Pankhurst was given a fine of ten shillings or a jail sentence of one week. Both girls promptly chose the prison sentence.

Emmeline Pankhurst, *My own Story*, pp. 47–8

31 A suffragette demonstration in Victoria Park, 1913

Comment

The Women's Social and Political Union was founded by Mrs. Pankhurst in 1903 to campaign for women's suffrage (or 'votes for women'). The suffragettes, as they became known, were unsuccessful in persuading the Liberal government of 1906 to introduce a Bill on their behalf. Not to be denied, they attracted attention to their cause by an amazing campaign of violence. They smashed windows, set property on fire, chained themselves to railings and went on hunger strike in prison — but did not finally win their case until 1918. This extract describes an unsuccessful attempt to gain support by peaceful means.

Questions

a. Why did the suffragettes launch a major campaign in 1905?
b. Why did they prefer to deal with the Liberal leaders rather than gain support among ordinary Liberal candidates?
c. Who was Sir Edward Grey?
d. Why did he ignore Annie Kenney's question?
e. What methods were used to silence the suffragettes at this meeting?
f. Why do you think the girls chose to go to prison?
g. What does this extract tell us about the qualities of the suffragettes?
h. Examine Plate 31. Judging by the inscriptions on the banner, what arguments did the suffragettes put forward to support their claims?

43 Lloyd George

Not having had the opportunity of close study of public affairs, he had picked up his history, economics and politics as he went along. . . . His fixed points were those which had been set in his mind when he was a poor lad in a Welsh village — a lively sympathy for all who suffered from poverty and social injustice; and a fervent Welsh nationalism, which afterwards expanded into a championship of all small nationalities. Beyond that he was frankly an opportunist. . . . He was never anxious or fearful; his courage never flagged in face of the most formidable dangers. 'The battle was his pastime' and he seemed to be marching through life, head high, to the strains of 'The Men of Harlech'.

On the platform he was beyond compare. No-one in our time could sway a great audience like Lloyd George. It was an exciting experience to sit by his side and watch the swiftly changing moods of five or six thousand people, packed in some vast hall to the doors and to the roof, as they answered to the magic of the skilful orator. Nature had endowed him with fine features and an expressive voice of silvery tone. . . . He was also gifted with a perennial flow of humour, highly original, that he himself enjoyed with so much gusto that it instantly infected all his hearers . . .

In Parliament Lloyd George was a most effective speaker, especially in a hot debate, and always drew a crowded House and dominated it. But a Parliamentary audience is naturally more discriminating and critical than a popular meeting. It likes a convincing argument; it resents errors of fact — and while Lloyd George was always anxious to be accurate, temperament sometimes defeated him; and it is inclined to scoff at flights into the picturesque. Although his political energy, his unfailing courage and his ready humour won him much success, I doubt whether he will take rank among the greatest of our parliamentarians . . .

Rt. Hon. Viscount Samuel, *Memoirs*, pp. 87–9

Comment

David Lloyd George was brought up in a small Welsh village by his uncle — the local cobbler. After attending the elementary school, he eventually became a solicitor before entering parliament in 1890. He quickly gained a reputation as a brilliant debater and an ardent opponent of the Boer War. As president of the Board of Trade in Campbell-Bannerman's Liberal government (1906–8), he showed remarkable skill in handling trade disputes with the unions. Then, in 1908, he became chancellor of the exchequer under Asquith.

Questions

a. What do we learn from this passage about Lloyd George's education?
b. What effect did his Welsh upbringing have on him later as a politician?
c. What natural gifts helped him to sway large audiences? Can you think of any great issues which he put to the electorate in this way?
d. Why was he less successful as a speaker in parliament?
e. Give an example of Lloyd George's opportunism.
f. What other personal qualities are referred to in this passage?

44 Irish Home Rule

The national demand, in plain and popular language, is simply this, that the government of every purely Irish affair shall be controlled by the public opinion of Ireland, and by that alone. We demand this self-government as a right. For us the Act of Union has no binding, moral or legal force. We regard it as our fathers regarded it before us, as a great criminal act of usurpation, carried by violence and by fraud. . . . Resistance to the Act of Union will always remain for us, so long as that Act lasts, a sacred duty . . . and we declare that no ameliorative reforms, no number of Land Acts, or Labourers Acts, or Education Acts, no redress of financial grievances, no material improvement or industrial development, can ever satisfy Ireland until Irish laws are made and administered upon Irish soil by Irishmen.

But our claim to self-government does not rest solely upon historic right and title. It rests also, fellow-citizens, upon the failure of the British Government in Ireland for the last one hundred years. . . . Take the test of population. While in every civilised country in Europe the population has increased . . . in Ireland, in the last sixty years, it has diminished by one-half. Take the test of civil liberty. There has been a Coercion Act for every year since the Union was passed, and there is today in existence a law which enables the Lord Lieutenant, at his arbitrary discretion, by a stroke of the pen, to suspend trial by jury, personal liberty, freedom of discussion, and the right to public meeting all over Ireland . . .

Take the test of the contentment of the people. There have been since the Union three insurrections, all of them suppressed in blood, with sacrifices untold in the prison cell and upon the scaffold. . . . Take the test of the prosperity of Ireland . . . it is the history of constantly-recurring famines every few years over a large portion of the west and north-west seaboard of the country. Take the question of industrial development. A history of industries deliberately suppressed by British Acts of Parliament, and not one finger lifted in the last hundred years to advance industrial prosperity. . . . Now such a record as that . . . cries aloud for vengeance.

John Redmond's speech, Dublin, 4 September 1907

32 Opposition to Sir Edward Carson's Ulster Volunteers. The Springtown Volunteers at rifle drill, 1914

Comment

Salisbury's policy of 'twenty years' resolute government' by the Conservatives had failed to solve the Irish problem. Indeed, frustrated by the loss of Gladstone's Home Rule Bills in 1886 and 1893, the Irish themselves were even more determined to secure their freedom. The feeling is well reflected in this speech by John Redmond, leader of the Irish Nationalist party in parliament. By 1911 the Liberal government was dependent on Irish votes to secure the passage of the Parliament Bill. (See Document 47.) Under these circumstances, Asquith promised Redmond a Home Rule Bill in return for their immediate support. When it eventually appeared, it unleashed a storm of opposition from Protestant Ulster, which wanted the Union to continue. Violence increased as 'the Ulster Volunteers' took arms to resist Home Rule by force.

Questions

a. On what two points did Redmond base his claim for Home Rule?
b. Why did he say that the Act of Union was not legally binding? Why had its original passing caused so much bitterness?
c. What was his attitude to previous British governments and the policies which they had attempted in Ireland?
d. Why do you think the population of Ireland had declined during the nineteenth century?

45 The Osborne Judgment, 1909

House of Commons, 22 November 1910

Mr. G. N. BARNES: I desire to ask the Prime Minister a question, of which I have given him private notice, namely, whether the Government have yet had the opportunity of discussing the further attitude to be adopted on the Osborne Judgment?

The PRIME MINISTER: I have already indicated the intention of the Government in regard to payment of Members and official election expenses. We shall further propose legislation empowering trade unions to include in their objects and organisation the provision of a fund for Parliamentary and municipal action and representation and kindred objects, and to combine for such purposes, provided that the opinion of the union is effectively ascertained, and that there shall be no compulsion upon any member to contribute to the fund . . .

Mr. ARTHUR HENDERSON: Arising out of the latter part of the Prime Minister's answer, are we to understand that no member being compelled to subscribe there is going to be some provisions for a member to contract out?

The PRIME MINISTER: There is no necessity for contracting out.

Mr. KEIR HARDIE: Can the right hon. Gentleman say . . . what is meant by no compulsion? Is a member to be free to reclaim the amount of his contribution which might be applied for political purposes?

The PRIME MINISTER: No, Sir. He is not to be penalised or in any way injuriously affected if he refuses to pay.

Mr. KEIR HARDIE: May I ask, in the case of those unions — which are in a large majority — where there is no special levy for political purposes, and where the Parliamentary fund is taken out of the general funds of the union, what is to be the procedure?

The PRIME MINISTER: . . . it shall become one of the lawful objects of trade unions to provide a fund — by which I mean a separate fund.

Mr. KEIR HARDIE: Does that mean specifically that the union shall not be free to use its ordinary funds for political purposes, and must a political fund be raised by means of a special levy?

The PRIME MINISTER: Yes. I think that follows.

Hansard, 1910, Vol. 20, p. 275

Comment

In 1904 the unions decided to build up the funds of the newly formed Labour Representation Committee (see Document 38) by imposing a political levy on their members. However in 1909 a man called Osborne, who was a Liberal, objected to this demand for money to finance the Labour party and sued his union, the Amalgamated Society of Railway Servants. He won his case. The appeal judges in the Lords ruled that trade union funds were not to be presented to political parties. This, of course, raised a real threat to the position of working-class M.P.s in parliament.

Questions

a. What new legal power did the prime minister propose to give to trade unions following the Osborne Judgment?
b. On what two conditions would that power be based?
c. What exactly is meant by 'contracting out'?
d. Who was Arthur Henderson? Did he eventually persuade the government on this point of contracting out? (Consult the terms of the Trade Unions Act, 1913.)
e. How would the unions be required to organise (i) their subscriptions, (ii) their expenditure?
f. In what other way did the government propose to make it easier for working-class men to sit in parliament? When did their proposal become law?

46 The People's Budget, 1909

Mr. Lloyd George introduced his Budget in a speech of four hours in length. His voice gave way in the middle of the performance, and there was an adjournment of half an hour. So great, however, was the interest in the proposals he was outlining that the House was crowded during the whole of the speech . . .

No Budget in pre-war days ever exposed so many vulnerable points of attack. It was bound to excite the bitter opposition of a large number of vested interests. The opposition of the Income-Tax payers would be incurred by the proposed increase in the tax. The liquor interests would fight the increase in the licence duties to the utmost of their powers. One brewer asserted that these increased licenses would mean ruin to half the brewers of the country! The City was up in arms against the increases in the Stamp Duties, and, of course, the landed interests were infuriated by the proposed land taxes. Next morning the Press took a Party view of the Budget. It was denounced in the Tory newspapers without reserve under such headings as 'The Red Flag Budget'. One thing everybody agreed upon, that the Budget was so controversial that it was doubtful if it would be carried without modification . . .

Outside the House of Commons the campaign for and against the Budget was carried on with great vigour. Mr. Lloyd George addressed great meetings in the country, in which he attacked the landlords with a violence which would have done credit to a communist agitator. The debates upon the Budget occupied seventy-three days of parliamentary time. . . . After its successful passage through the House of Commons Mr. Lloyd George's Budget was sent to the House of Lords. After six days' debate in that Chamber it was rejected by 350 votes to 75. This debate and division were the most remarkable which ever took place in their Lordships' House. On each day of the debate, at the opening of the sitting, there were long queues of peers taking the oath who had never put in an attendance during this Parliament. Never had there been such an attendance of peers in the long life of this institution.

Philip Viscount Snowden, *An Autobiography*, Vol. I, pp. 195–204

33 'Budget—
"Did you say that
you wouldn't
swallow me
without mincing?"
Lord Lansdowne—
"No, sir—
please, sir—I never
said *mincing*, I
might have said
wincing."'

Comment

As chancellor of the exchequer in 1909, Lloyd George was faced with an enormous problem of raising extra revenue. Money had to be found to pay for the eight new 'Dreadnoughts' ordered by the navy, as well as labour exchanges, road improvements and children's allowances planned by the government. In his budget he found the necessary cash largely out of rich men's pockets. The wealthy classes seethed with indignation and the predominantly Conservative House of Lords rejected the budget. It was against all parliamentary tradition for the Lords to turn down a finance bill. Parliament was dissolved and Asquith put the issue to the country at the election.

Questions

a. Which groups of people opposed the budget? What had they in common?
b. Why did Snowden call the debate in the Lords 'the most remarkable' ever to have taken place there?
c. Why do you think the Lords showed so much interest in this debate? Were they right to reject the budget?
d. How does this extract illustrate the personal qualities of Lloyd George?
e. Examine Plate 33. Who are the two characters in the cartoon? What do they represent? Why is the one on the right so large?

47 The Parliament Act, 1911

The Government lost no time in introducing a resolution dealing with the House of Lords question. This was afterwards embodied in the Parliament Bill. This Bill provided that the House of Lords would have no control at all over national finance; the House of Commons would have the last word in all matters of legislation. The maximum duration of Parliament would be reduced from seven years to five years.

In October my wife and I went to America to fulfil an engagement to give a short series of lectures. We were in Pittsburg when the news came of the breakdown of the Conference and the Government's decision to dissolve Parliament. The American newspapers gave alarmist reports of the political crisis in England, and one evening newspaper in Pittsburg came out with a front-page scarehead in letters an inch deep: 'Revolution in England! King George in flight?' The only foundation for the startling news that the King was in flight was, if I remember rightly, that he was on his way from Balmoral to London to be in close touch with his Ministers. I had to make arrangements to return to England at once . . .

When I emerged from the station [at Blackburn] to my amazement the great square outside was packed by a dense crowd. . . . The route through the principal streets to the market-place was marked by scenes of unprecedented enthusiasm. . . . It was a great start for our Election campaign, which a week later ended in a triumphant victory. This contest was fought exclusively on the House of Lords issue.

For the second time within twelve months the country had decided the issue of The Peers *versus* The People. The Government had received a very definite mandate from the country to place the Parliament Bill upon the Statute Book with the least possible delay. The Liberals and Labour and the Nationalists combined had a majority of 126 over the Unionists. Owing to unpreparedness, the Labour Party put forward only 56 candidates at this General Election (December 1910), and 42 were returned. . . . It had been very greatly hampered by a recent decision of the House of Lords which had declared it to be illegal for trade unionists to spend the funds of their organisations on political work.

Philip Viscount Snowden, *An Autobiography*, Vol. I, pp. 211–13

THE DAWN OF HOPE.

Mr. LLOYD GEORGE'S National Health Insurance Bill provides for the insurance of the Worker in case of Sickness.

34 Liberal Party poster, 1911   **Support the Liberal Government**
in their policy of
SOCIAL REFORM.

Comment

The defeat of the budget marked the climax of a bitter struggle between the Commons and the Lords which had been developing since 1906. The Conservative Lords had rejected or seriously amended a number of important bills sent up to them by the democratically-elected Liberal government. After the first election of 1910, the Liberals and their supporters were again returned with a large majority. Under the weight of this pressure, the Lords finally passed the budget. However Asquith, who was quite determined to reduce the power of the Lords, now introduced the Parliament Bill. It nevertheless took a second election to persuade the Lords to agree.

Questions

a. In what way was the power of the House of Lords restricted by the Parliament Act?
b. Why was the life of parliament reduced from seven to five years?
c. What would be the advantages and disadvantages of reducing it even further?
d. Why had the government decided to dissolve parliament and call a second election within a year? What was the main issue at the election?

48 Naval Armaments

House of Commons, Wednesday, 22 March 1911

Mr. YERBURGH asked what will be the strength of the German Fleet in battleships distinguished as 'Dreadnoughts' and pre-'Dreadnoughts' on the completion of the Navy Act of 1900 . . .

Mr. McKENNA: The German Fleet Law with its amendments provides for thirty-eight battleships. In 1920 Germany will possess thirty-nine of these ships, of which twenty-two will be 'Dreadnoughts' . . .

Mr. MIDDLEMORE asked how many armoured ships have been provided for the British Fleet in the financial years 1906–7 to 1911–12 inclusive: and how many have in the same period been provided for the fleets of Germany, the United States, France, Russia, Italy, Austria and Japan?

Mr. McKENNA: The following are the figures asked for by the hon. Member . . .

Great Britain	26
Germany	22
United States	12
France	11
Russia	4
Italy	5
Austro-Hungary	7
Japan	4

Mr. MIDDLEMORE: Do not these figures show that we have not maintained the two-Power standard against Germany plus any naval Power in the world? . . . How many ships of the 'Dreadnought' type were now in commission for the British Navy, and how many are at present in dockyard hands?

Mr. McKENNA: There are twelve ships of 'Dreadnought' type now in commission. Of these, four are in dockyard hands and one other, the *Indefatigable*, was commissioned on 24th February last, and is now in contractors' hands re-making steam pipe joints.

Mr. MIDDLEMORE: . . . does the right hon. Gentleman consider that twenty-nine ships as against the German twenty-one in 1914 gives us an adequate margin?

Hansard, 1911, Vol. 23, p. 993

35 'Poker and Tongs; or, how we've got to play the game. Kaiser—"I go three *Dreadnoughts*" John Bull—"Well, just to show there's no ill-feeling, I raise you three."'

Comment

Sir John Fisher (the first sea lord) completely revised the navy's ship-building methods to take account of attacks by the new torpedoes. In 1906, therefore, the first 'Dreadnought' was launched — an armour-plated battleship with ten 12-inch guns and a speed of 21 knots. This rendered obsolete all previous battleships and cruisers. Germany quickly copied the new design — and the race for naval armaments was on.

Questions

a. What exactly was a 'Dreadnought'?
b. What had the German Navy Law proposed in 1900?
c. What did Mr. Middlemore mean by Britain's 'two-Power standard'?
d. Compare the number of armed ships built between 1906 and 1912 by the members of the Triple Entente with those of the Triple Alliance.
e. What remark in particular indicates the real concern felt in Britain about the German threat to her naval supremacy?
f. Examine Plate 35. Explain the meaning of this cartoon.